Are you a
PrimeTime
woman?
I have a
gift for
you...

FREE.PRIMETIMEJUJU.COM

HOT FLASHES CARPOOLS & Dirty MARTINIS

JUJU HOOK

AB

ARMSTRONG BARTOW PRESS

CALIFORNIA

Publisher's Cataloging-In-Publication Data
(Prepared by The Donohue Group, Inc.)

Names: Hook, Juju.
Title: Hot flashes, carpools & dirty martinis : the quintessential guide for turning midlife into primetime / Juju Hook.
Other Titles: Hot flashes, carpools and dirty martinis
Description: Carlsbad, CA : Armstrong Bartow Press, [2017] | Includes bibliographical references.
Identifiers: ISBN 9780999352311 | ISBN 9780999352304 (ebook) | ISBN 9780999352328 (audiobook)
Subjects: LCSH: Self-actualization (Psychology) in middle age. | Self-actualization (Psychology) in women. | Middle-aged women--Psychology. | Midlife crisis. | Hook, Juju.
Classification: LCC BF724.65.S44 H66 2017 (print) | LCC BF724.65.S44 (ebook) | DDC 155.6/6--dc23

Printed by Armstrong Bartow Press in the United States

Armstrong Bartow Press
2911 Sondra Court
Carlsbad, CA 92009

Paperback ISBN: 978-0-9993523-1-1
Ebook ISBN: 978-0-9993523-0-4
Audiobook ISBN: 978-0-9993523-2-8

Quantity sales. Special discounts are available on quantity purchases by corporations, associations, and others. Special programs including live Q&A sessions with the author are also available for book clubs. For details, contact the publisher at info@ArmstrongBartowPress.com.

The author has attempted to recreate events, locales and conversations from memories. In order to maintain their anonymity, in some names of individuals and places have changed, as well as identifying characteristics and details such as physical properties, occupations, and places of residence.
Although the author and publisher have made every effort to ensure that the information in this book was correct at press time, the author and publisher do not assume and hereby disclaim any liability to any party for any loss, damage, or disruption caused by errors or omissions, whether such errors or omissions result from negligence, accident, or any other cause.
This book is not intended as a substitute for the advice of psychiatrists or physicians. The reader should regularly consult a physician in matters relating to his/her health and/or a mental health expert particularly with respect to any symptoms that may require diagnosis or medical attention.

Printed in the United States of America.

For Jan
Who saw the best version of me
And then loved me patiently while I became her.
I love you.

Table of Contents

PART I

Prime Time

Jump in, let's go
Lay back, enjoy the show
Everybody gets high, everybody gets low
These are the days when anything goes
Everyday is a winding road
I get a little bit closer
Everyday is a faded sign
I get a little bit closer feeling fine

— SHERYL CROW

CHAPTER 1

My Jerry Springer Show Morning

I was 35 when our son, Christian, took his first breath. We had him late by parenting industry standards. That put all of us in the unenviable positions, years later, of me beginning early menopause just around the time Christian was reaching puberty. Menopause and puberty go together like beer and ice cream. For about a year, our house was constantly in a low state of rumble, right on the edge of serious upset.

One morning when Christian was 13, we had a Jerry Springer Show episode in our house. It left me sitting on the edge of his bed, with him having just climbed out his second-story window into a rainstorm. And me with my head in my hands, pajamas smelly and soaked, asking myself through the olive-tinged fog of a martini hangover, "How the hell did we get here?"

This episode also launched me into a new career.

I had awakened that Friday morning to the sound of rain pounding on our clay-tile roof. The pounding in my head was an echo. The night before, I'd made a bold choice to forego the Pinot Noir I'd come to love (and trust) with dinner, and instead enjoy a couple of dirty martinis. My rationale was entirely sound. The recent shift in my hormones had played a cruel trick on my relationship with velvety red wines. The wine still went down like a charm, but the days that followed—no matter how small the quantity consumed—had become painful, muddled, gloomy, and unproductive. I'd wisely decided to try something different.

I'd also hot-flashed through the night, in a repeated cycle that was longer but every bit as reliable as the cycle of waves that tumbled onto our beloved Ponto State Beach down the street. The cycle began the moment I fell into my deepest sleep, and repeated once every 20 minutes until the 6:00 a.m. alarm. Each time, I'd be pulled out of a serene and glassy slumber by an internal heat wave that would rise and crest gloriously at what felt like a thousand degrees. Then I would kick off the covers in a fit and drift back to sleep. Moments later, I'd be woken again—drenched from sweat, totally exposed, teeth chattering—as the wave crashed, right at the edge of my sanity.

One of the few pursuits more frustrating than struggling to sleep through hot flashes is fighting to wake a pubescent boy. So while the morning alarm marked the end of one battle, it signaled the beginning of the next. My body was awake. But my sense of humor would need a while to catch up.

Groggy and preoccupied, I headed downstairs to the kitchen, an angry and insistent voice in my head screaming, "COFFEE, COFFEE, COFFEE!" As I walked off the last step, my bare foot landed squarely in a plushly carpeted puddle of freezing water.

It was on like fucking Donkey Kong.

My in-laws were in the house that morning. They were wintering with us, having recently flown in from Germany, which helped to create the perfect storm. The entire situation was intensified by the actual storm that had seized San Diego after months of drought, and by my lack of attention to the sticky slurry of leaves and dirt that had clogged our rain gutters in the meantime.

The small lake that snapped me out of my stupor was about three inches deep and ran the length of our hallway. It took me only 10 frantic seconds to discover the source. At the rate of approximately one bucket per minute, water from outside was gushing through the vent into the laundry room, just on the other side of my in-law's bedroom wall.

While my screams of "SHIT, SHIT, SHIT!" were not a terribly elegant way to wake the sleeping Germans, they were effective. In a split second, we were all standing in the hallway, our pajama bottoms soaked, staring at one another like passengers on a sinking ship.

German in-laws, as beautiful chance would have it, are the best possible houseguests in a moment of non-existential crisis. They know what to do when shit hits the fan. And they are unbelievably efficient at getting it done.

In a literal flash, my father-in-law was outside assessing the lake that had formed along the side of the house. Seconds later, he was on the roof (torrential downpour be damned), scooping leaves from the gutter. My mother-in-law grabbed a broom and, before I could shout a single obscenity more, began sweeping water from the laundry room into the garage. I gathered towels, rugs, and finally the dirty laundry, to sop up what she couldn't sweep.

Nearly 45 minutes whizzed by before I realized I'd forgotten to wake the sleeping teen.

Today was an especially bad day for a late awakening—Mastery Learning Day. This would set the stage for an emotional terrorist attack from which we wouldn't recover until hours later. And for an existential crisis for me that took me the better part of two years to clean up. (Sadly, my German in-laws had no efficient solution for this.)

Mastery Learning Day was a hallowed occasion and somewhat new to our family. The process at The Grauer School, where Christian was a new seventh-grader at the time, works like this. The students are required to set a Mastery Learning Level in each class of no lower than 80%. They must complete every assignment at or above that grade level, even if it means reworking it several times. Using this system, the students master subjects before moving on. On the last day of the quarter—dubbed Mastery Learning Day—they must submit portfolios for each class, organized to include every assignment from the prior 13 weeks.

There's a tasty carrot for the kids on this special day. If they present their fully organized portfolios and obtain signatures from every teacher, they earn a half day off school to muck around and celebrate. Otherwise, they're required to hang out at school and finish whatever assignments are missing or not up to par, while their friends are out having a blast.

This was to be our family's second experience with Mastery Learning Day. The first had been a veritable shit show, filled with drama and tears. Christian was upset as well. He had to complete three hours of make-up math work while the other kids hung at the beach, and he sulked for days afterwards.

If you've ever met any 13-year-old boys, you know that "organized" is a wholly unnatural state for these perpetually preoccupied creatures. So you can imagine my trepidation as I—soaked, sleep-deprived, still in fight-or-flight mode, and without my morning coffee—climbed the stairs to his room, knowing that today organization would be the key to the kingdom.

I threw open the door, switched on the light, and shouted, "Christian, WAKE UP—we're late! We had a flood! Get your stuff. No time for a shower!"

You know that little infographic they always show in management and leadership courses? The one that indicates 55% of communication is body language, 38% is tone of voice, and only 7% is represented by the words you say? On that morning, what I meant to communicate was, "Let's move quickly, sweetheart. We really need to work as a team here." Instead, what I communicated was more like, "Do what I say. OUR LIVES ARE IN DANGER. And don't fuck with me, because I'm totally deranged!"

Christian leapt out of bed swinging. He was pissed at me. More importantly, he was pissed at himself. He'd chosen You-Tube over math the night before. He'd opted in advance for a morning crisis, a manipulation I'd allowed him to hone over months of practice. And he immediately took me hostage.

"SERIOUSLY, Mom?! You said you'd wake me up! I need your help with algebra! I will NEVER finish this by myself! I wish we'd never moved here. This is all your fault. I HATE YOU."

From there, the situation just escalated. More shouting. More swearing. Rage on both sides. Christian's chin jutted forward as he glared at me and taunted me with his eyes. My voice escalated as my control over the situation—and my emotions—slipped away. My in-laws stood in the hallway, mouths agape, in shock and awe at what had become of our once-normal family in the nine months since they'd last visited America.

In a moment of fury, I grabbed Christian by his shirt, and pulled him close to my face as I spewed angry words.

Then he was gone. Out the window. Into the storm.

The feeling of shame and remorse that hit me was instant and visceral. I couldn't breathe. I couldn't cry. And I couldn't imagine how I'd gotten to this place.

But I knew two things for certain: 1) We had crossed a boundary we were never meant to cross, and could never allow ourselves to cross again, and 2) The once-effective and simplistic approach of parenting through power had reached a bitter end. It was time for a change.

I called my husband, Jan, to tell him what had happened. At the time, he was working and living weekdays in Yuma, Arizona, about a three-hour drive from our San Diego house. We'd devised a new arrangement, and we were still trying to figure out how to make it work. Jan was painfully familiar with both my hormonal hysteria and our son's growing sense of entitlement, and I secretly suspected he was relieved to be 180 miles away from both.

"We had a flood," I said, breathlessly. "Christian and I had a huge fight. He ran away. He climbed out the window. It's pouring. School starts in 30 minutes, and it's Mastery Learning Day."

Not even a "Good morning."

Jan paused for a deep breath before he replied, calm and self-assured. "Do NOT go after him. He cannot threaten us, in our own home, every time there's a conflict."

"It's pouring, Jan. It's freezing!"

"Julia, you're in San Diego. It's not freezing. It's 60 degrees. He's fully dressed. No one ever died from rain. And really, where's he gonna run? To the land of free internet?"

I knew Jan was right. His emotions, especially in moments of crisis, had always seemed unnaturally stable to me. In fact, Jan would have never called this moment a crisis at all.

"You need to pull it together," he said. "Calm down. Take a shower. Get yourself dressed. And when he comes back, just don't speak to him about it again. Don't say another word. Drive him to school in silence, and drop him off. Bring the drama to an end. Just let him think about it for the day. Keep your cool. Can you do that?"

"I can," I responded. "I will."

We both knew his request was akin to asking a woodpecker not to peck.

Off to the shower I went, my stomach bound in knots, and my skin coated with the sweaty, sticky stench of shame and muddy floodwater.

On the way down the hall, I passed my in-laws and gave them a lame, shaky smile. "Do NOT go after him," I ordered. "Jan was very specific about this. Let him come back on his own."

As I turned to walk away, I knew that before hot water would hit my flesh, my mother-in-law would be out the door with a dry towel, a hard-boiled egg, a piece of freshly baked bread, and a hug for her grandson. I suspect someone, somewhere, has completed a fascinating study about why the most pragmatic and firm parents turn to a pile of mush the day their grandchildren are born. My European in-laws serve as proof that this is, at the very least, a trans-continental phenomenon.

By the time I had my shoes on, Christian was back in the house. Not a word was spoken as we walked to the car and drove the 20 minutes to school. We were both exhausted, embarrassed, and relieved at the reprieve. The spectacle was over.

Until a phone call about three hours later, from the founder of The Grauer School himself, Stuart Grauer.

I like Stuart. We chose Christian's school because of his alternative yet wise and proven beliefs about small-school education. That said, even at the age of 50, I fear I might piss my pants any time a school principal says my name aloud. It transports me right back to the first day of first grade at Indian Run Elementary School. I peed my pants during the Pledge of Allegiance and had to go to the principal's office. I waited patiently in my new school dress with nothing underneath but a cool breeze, while the school secretary dried my panties in the dryer. It's highly likely that I have post-traumatic stress disorder from that incident.

"Julia," Stuart said, "do you have a minute?"

"Sure!" I replied, a little too eagerly, my voice cracking.

"I spent some time with Christian today. And he seems pretty stressed out."

My automatic thought-generator switched into high gear.

So he told.

He took it all to school.

It's out in the open.

This man thinks I'm a monster.

I AM a monster.

What the fuck was I thinking, grabbing Christian like that?

How did he get around to discussing this with Stuart in the first place?

They must have noticed he was wet.

I wonder if everyone at school knows.

Are they kicking us out?

That little shit.

Holy shit.

Are we in deep shit?

"Yes," I replied. "We've had some power struggles at home. It hasn't been an easy few months between Christian and me."

"What's going on?" Stuart asked, without the slightest hint of judgment.

"He won't do his work, Stuart. He won't apply himself. He won't study for tests. He has the potential, but he just won't step up. He's not happy about being at a new school, and he's just refusing to participate."

There. The cat was out of the bag. I was suddenly a monster and a snitch. I had ratted out my son to his school principal, had thrown him under the bus in three seconds flat, only to save myself. It wouldn't be long now before I was hittin' a crack pipe and calling the cops on him for assault and battery. Parenting is a slippery slope, my friend. And this was a terribly rainy day.

"Julia, what are you so afraid of?"

Then the floodgates opened. For real.

"I'm afraid he won't be successful. I'm afraid he's never gonna apply himself to anything. What if he isn't accepted by a good college? What if he flunks out? I know it's your policy to let the kids experience failure—to let them take responsibility for their own stuff. But what if he never does? How far are you willing to let him fall, Stuart? All the way to the street?"

I've been accused of many things in my life. Underreacting has never been one of them.

"He's in the seventh grade, Julia." His voice was more kind and patient than I deserved. "And you can't parent from fear. You can only parent from love. If you continue like this, Christian will come to believe that your love for him is conditional on some kind of performance. You'll be locked in a power struggle forever. He has to find his own way. Kids need to find their own motivation. It needs to come from inside."

"But what if it doesn't?" I retorted, a little more desperately than I'd meant to. "What if he never rises? What if he never fulfills his potential? What if he just skates by forever? And he never lives out his purpose and his dreams?"

Next came a pause longer and more uncomfortable than any I could remember enduring.

"Julia, I want to say something to you that I wouldn't say to most other parents—because I don't think every parent could handle it, and I think most parents might be angry. But I know you, and I believe you'll understand this. I don't think this is about Christian. I think this about you."

I'd been exposed. My days as a closet narcissist were over. The principal could see it. And he had known me for all of three months.

He continued. "I'd like to make a suggestion, if you're open to it."

"Of course," I said. What else could I say?

"Go do something *you're* afraid of. You've put way too much of your time and focus on Christian. You need something to do. He's 13 now. He doesn't need you in his life—in that way—anymore. Take this energy and apply it to yourself. Go find something to do that terrifies you."

You're holding that thing in your hands right now.

AN ERROR IN PROGRAMMING

I'm not much of a believer in life-changing moments. I hear people talk about them. I read about a-ha experiences that turn couch-potato cupcake addicts into green-juice-drinking personal trainers. About brush-with-death encounters that make spiritual gurus out of material girls. About remarkable discoveries that elevate millennials from their moms' basements on a Thursday to private villas in Belize on Monday.

I must admit, I've always been secretly jealous of that kind of whip-bang reversal of emotional (and sometimes literal) fortune. My own personal development is more of an osmosis kind of deal. I arrive at realizations, then—with equal parts hard work, humility, and grace—assimilate what I've learned and pop out on the other side as Juju 2.0. (I'm probably up to version 4.7 by now.)

So when Stuart Grauer outed me that day, it wasn't so much an instant sea-change as a catalyst for one. An awakening. The moment of my most meaningful realization ever: I was in PrimeTime.

I had spent my whole damn life preparing for this time slot. I was finally at my highest potential. I was experienced. I had honed my craft. I was wise and brazen and *ready*. But I was living my life like a rerun of *Laverne and Shirley*.

14

In the moment of that realization, I took my first step on a journey. At first I set out on a path to change my own midlife situation. But it quickly became much more significant.

Over the past three years, I've discovered that most women my age have bought into an outdated and entirely inaccurate definition of "midlife." We have allowed ourselves to be branded, and we have played a huge role in propagating the myths associated with that brand. To some extent, almost every midlife woman I've met has downplayed, missed out on, given away, or disregarded her own PrimeTime. And we've all done it for remarkably similar reasons.

In short, we believe shit that just isn't true. Then we act—or refuse to act—because of it.

At a turning point in my journey, it became my life's mission to rebrand middle age for all women. I became obsessed with showing middle-aged women the truth about their potential, potency, viability, and wisdom. I focused on showing the rest of the world that they're completely wrong about us.

I became fixated on shutting down the bullshit, and entirely consumed with the idea of starting a PrimeTime revolution.

If you are a woman over 40, and you've ever felt irrelevant or invisible, this book is for you. If you're facing a transition, and you're wondering what the hell to do next, then this book is for you. If you've ever felt shut out because you feel that something you want to have, do, say, or be is "inappropriate for a woman your age," then this book is for you. If, with each passing decade, you feel less passionate, less confident, and less sexy, then this book is for you. If the world has told you that middle age is a step down, and that from here on out your days will only be worse, then this book is for you.

Because every single bit of that is a crock of shit.

But before I delve too deep into all of that, I need to introduce you to the concept of PrimeTime, and show you why you're in it...right at this precise moment.

CHAPTER 2

Life in Dayparts

PROGRAMMING BY HELEN

From the time I was seven—until I was about 11—every Saturday morning my mom would drop me off at my grandparents' yellow house in Grandview, Ohio. The 1950s bungalow was neatly nestled in a row of pastel duplexes with cement steps leading to wide front porches. I would stay there until late morning on Sunday.

My grandma, Helen, was a fucking baller. From her, I learned most everything I know about badassery. Helen took zero shit from anyone, and gave zero fucks about what anyone else wanted or thought. She retired (at the age of 62) from her career as an accountant at the Abex–Dennison hydraulics company. On that very day, she withdrew her profit-sharing money and bought herself a light-green Pontiac Grand Prix with a four-barrel V-8 engine and white vinyl interior. She drove it like a bat out of hell.

Helen owned her own bowling ball, bag, and glove. She drank beer from a Pilsner glass. She frequently responded to questions with "Oh, for Christ's sake." She chain-smoked Carlton cigarettes, which she bought by the carton. And the candy-bowl-sized ashtray in her Grand Prix overflowed with butts stained the color of Brach's cherry sourballs by her lipstick. When she railed on my grandpa, he would say, "Helen, who rattled your chain?"

In retrospect, the house at 1543 West 3rd Avenue was a schoolhouse for me. I learned some of the most valuable and poignant lessons of my life there. I learned that margarine is bullshit, and the only reason eggs and toast taste good at all is because of real salted butter. I learned that the main symptom of Alzheimer's disease is nonsense. And on the morning my grandpa showed up to the kitchen table to work his crossword puzzle wearing two full sets of false teeth, I learned that nonsense could be both terrifying and hilarious at the same time.

As I slept all those Saturday nights on one of the twin beds in my grandma's room, I learned that some marriages are a power struggle. That one person always has the upper hand. And that certain kinds of transgressions are followed by a lifetime of punishment.

But the most practical lesson I learned—the one that would serve as the foundation for my future career in advertising and branding—was the concept of television dayparts.

What I know now is that television networks divide the day into parts—each consisting of a specific number of hours. Within each of those dayparts, they air programs that are designed to attract an *extremely specific* group of consumers. Then they sell advertising space to companies who want to place their products in front of those exact folks.

As a kid, in front of a giant console, I instinctively understood that some dayparts were a full-blown joyride and others were an unmitigated bore.

My Saturday mornings, like for most kids in my era, started with cartoons. *Bugs Bunny*, *Scooby Doo*, *Shazam*, and *Isis* dominated the Breakfast/Early Morning daypart, and I was glued to the screen. Late morning, my grandma would take me to the grocery store (where we always bought a pound of chipped ham and a package of egg buns), then to the Gold Circle for household items (where we always bought a bottle of full-codeine Nyquil for my grandpa).

After shopping, Helen relaxed on her scratchy, red plaid couch during Weekend Daytime programming. In a living room darkened by heavy gold drapes and a perpetual cloud of smoke, she watched professional bowling, brought to her by Brunswick.

When Weekend Daytime was over, my grandma would sew. Long before Hillary spawned a nation, Helen made pantsuits for me on her Singer sewing machine. I wore them to school as early as the first grade.

She would pin the tissue paper from the Butterick patterns onto polyester that we'd chosen together from the sale bolts at the local fabric store. My job was to hand her the stick pins, which I pulled from a pin-cushion the shape and color of the tomatoes my grandpa grew next to the driveway. Helen would flawlessly trim the pieces into complicated shapes using heavy metal shears I was forbidden to touch. I can remember the sound of the dull side of the shears sliding along the dining room table as she leaned into her project.

What I remember most, though, is how she stood over the ironing board and pressed the inside seams of each piece before sewing them together. A Carlton would hang off her bottom lip as she talked, an inch of ash dangling precariously over my pantsuit-to-be, but miraculously never falling. During those ironing sessions, my grandma taught me that I was a baller, too.

She'd say, "Julia, do not wear dresses. They make you look weak. You should always wear pants, like the men. You're every bit as smart as them, and a better leader. Don't take any shit from them. They have their heads up their asses."

After our sewing/motivational sessions, Helen would make her way back to the TV for the evening news and the Prime Access daypart, which stretched from 7:00 to 8:00 p.m. My grandpa, Bob, would join her. God, how they loved Prime Access. It featured *The Lawrence Welk Show*, which was a long, painful musical yawn. Each week when the bubbles began to flow, signifying the end of the program, I began to feel a rush.

Hee Haw came next, which was tolerable. I got an occasional laugh between segments, when Barbie Benton would jump out in her booby-farm-girl outfit with a pitchfork while Roy and Buck lobbed some real zingers at her. But for the most part, the jokes were over my head.

For me, the Prime Access daypart was like Purgatory. I was stuck there, repenting my sins, until I would be welcomed into the heaven that was PrimeTime.

In the early 70s, CBS ruled PrimeTime on Saturday nights. It began at 8:00 p.m., with *All in the Family*, which cracked my grandma's and grandpa's shit *up*. Together they laughed out loud, but each from a different perspective. As Archie Bunker told his wife, Edith, to "Stifle it" and called his son-in-law "Meathead," my grandpa lived vicariously through him. But Helen? She channeled Archie.

I loved *All in the Family* too. Not because I found it funny, but because it served as the gateway to my personal freedom. As soon as the show was over, my grandparents would leave me alone with the TV while they set up the dining room for Pinochle and highballs with Mildred and Harold, who lived on the other side of the duplex.

Mildred drank gin and smelled of it 24/7. She smoked non-filter Camels, and had her hair in rollers so often that I assumed it to be her actual hairstyle. She snorted when she laughed, called me "kid," and said, "Ya know what I mean?" at the end of every sentence.

Harold was a retired military guy who was in one of those man clubs where he wore a fez. He smoked cigars and had little use for me. The only enduring memory I have of Harold is that when he died, Mildred found that he had stashed paper lunch sacks filled with cash all over their house. She and my grandma used the money to go on a cruise. That tropical vacation was the only time I ever remember them leaving the house, aside from our Saturday morning grocery trips.

While my grandma and Harold teamed up against my grandpa and Mildred for Pinochle, I would lie in front of the console TV and watch *The Mary Tyler Moore Show*, *The Bob Newhart Show*, and *The Carol Burnett Show*. (Helen's console was a showpiece. About three feet high, finished in walnut shellac, the unit featured a 24-inch screen flanked by 2 speakers covered in saffron polyester. It had knobs the size of my 7-year-old fists.) I was also allowed to pick up the three-pound receiver on the sunflower-colored wall phone in the kitchen, make a rotary-dialed call to Tony's Pizza, and order my very own Small Pepperoni.

I would answer the door myself, and pay the delivery boy with a $5 bill (including the tip) which my grandma instructed me to pull from her billfold. The pizza was cut into squares, and I would ration them throughout PrimeTime, eating the inside pieces first. I saved the scrumptiously crusty edge pieces for the last hour, when I howled with laughter as Carol Burnett, Vicki Lawrence, Tim Conway, and Harvey Korman struggled not to.

I waited all damn day for PrimeTime. And it never, ever disappointed.

WE NEVER EVEN HAD A CHANCE

You can imagine my shock, horror, and even shame when I realized, at 47, that I'd reached PrimeTime in my life—that coveted spot between 8:00 and 11:00 p.m.—but I was still airing programming suitable for Prime Access. I had never even given myself a *chance*. Because I was too afraid my pilot would flop, my studio audience would be bored to tears, or my ratings would totally suck. Even more than that, at 47, I also believed that my time was up. I was irrelevant, past my heyday. I believed I was diminished in some real way.

In the three years since Stuart compelled me to challenge my fears, I've made it my mission to talk with hundreds of women who are also in PrimeTime. I have...

- Coached scores of female entrepreneurs.
- Sat with moms of teens on snowboarding trips.
- Marched with thousands of women to the City Hall in Los Angeles.
- Gabbed through umpteen happy hours.
- Led an online group for women looking to access their inner badasses.
- And answered countless emails, blog post comments, and Facebook private messages.

And you know what I discovered about PrimeTime women?

1. Whatever terrifies us the most, or we've put off the longest, is what we ought to be doing in PrimeTime. If it scares and excites you, then it should your Prime-Time mission.

2. Nearly every woman who is pussyfootin' around PrimeTime has succumbed to some form of the same fate that beset me: She's never given herself a *chance*.

3. Almost all of these women accepted this fate because they believed what the world told them about middle age. They allowed themselves to be defined by what is, essentially, complete and utter bullshit.

My husband, Jan, set out to be a competitive Ironman during his PrimeTime. He swims 2.4 miles, then cycles 112, then runs 26.2. I say he's a competitive Ironman, because he doesn't just want to finish; he races to win. Every season, he sets out to play with the big boys at the World Championship race in Kona, Hawaii. In order to do that, he must earn a slot by taking first place in his age division at a local Ironman event.

It's a masochistic kind of goal that requires commitment far beyond anything a normal human would consider. And Jan is an amateur, which means no prize money, no sponsors, no TV time or magazine write-ups. It comes with no glory at all, except for that which comes from within and bragging rights.

And some medals, which do look kinda bitchin'.

One night years ago, as we lay together in bed after he'd had a six-hour workout day and I'd had a pedicure and happy hour, I turned to him with genuine wonder and asked, "Is it *fun* for you?"

He leaned up on his elbow to look at me, and rolled his eyes upward as he considered the question. I could feel the heat coming off of him the way it always does after long work-outs. His voice was hoarse from a hard cardio effort.

"Fun?" he replied. "I wouldn't say it's actually *fun*. But I do enjoy it. I enjoy seeing how far I can push my own body. I like the feeling of going straight to that edge."

What Jan enjoys is giving himself a *chance*.

So why don't we women give ourselves a chance that same way in PrimeTime? Why don't we fully lean in to our dreams? Why wasn't I waking up every day and saying, "Hot damn, it's my burning desire to be an author. So I'd better sit down today—and every other day—and see how many words I can write! I'm going to make those words my *bitch*!"

Instead, I said whiney crap to myself like, "If SHE can write a book, I can write a book. I've always had a book in me. But I'm not ready just yet. I'll wait for Christian to graduate, then I can focus on me."

Or "I'd sure love to write a book, but I'm too busy. I don't have the luxury of time to myself."

Or "This job is all I can handle right now. It must be nice to have the money to spend time on a project like that. And anyway, I'm probably not good enough to be published."

At one point, I even convinced myself I couldn't write a book because I was 25 pounds overweight, as though the exertion from typing would be a risk to my heart!

Being a published author was *my* big, terrifying dream. But *your* big goal could be anything. I'm talking about every kind of endeavor, adventure, or aspiration ever considered "big" by a PrimeTime woman.

Within the past two years, I met a woman who wants to be a girls' basketball coach, but she thinks she's too old and unqualified, because she'd spent the past 15 years "just" raising kids. I've worked with a wonderfully talented performance artist who feels damaged by the losses she's experienced in life and is afraid to make a living from her art. Another has a burning desire to heal the world through essential oils, and has completed comprehensive training, but is 100% convinced that she can't launch her business until she's divorced and has moved out of the house. I know a whip-smart ad exec who yearns to be a political activist, but is proficient and profitable in advertising, so she feels like her dream is irresponsible. Or how about the woman who's been married for more than 20 years to an alcoholic husband, and can't even figure out what she wants, so she simply wants for nothing?

The list goes on and on and on…

PRIMETIME IN OUR TIME

In the United States, from 2000 to 2014, the proportion of first births to women aged 30 to 34 increased 28%, and those among women over 35 went up 23%. That number should continue to grow as the miracles of modern fertility medicine provide women the opportunity to have children well into their 40s. Before my husband and I were kicked out of Lamaze class for bad behavior, I was the youngest woman in the group, at age 34.

(If you must know, he fell asleep during *my* deep breathing exercise, and when I shook him to remind him that this was about *me*, he shouted, "Isn't it *always*?!" Naturally, I whacked him with a pillow. After 60 minutes of our senseless bickering and cutting up, the instructor showed us politely to the door, and suggested that Lamaze might not be the best technique for a couple like us.)

You know what all of these statistics mean? Loads of perimenopausal and menopausal women are raising teenagers. Thousands of women are experiencing massive hormonal shifts while their kids are experiencing shifts in the other direction.

We're the first generation of women to experience this phenomenon. My mom had three kids by the time she was 22, and her story was the norm in the late 50s. All told, she raised seven children. She enjoys a serious chuckle over my "one-kid problems." She laughs even harder at my constant struggle to "do parenting right."

She told me, "Honey, when I was your age, the section at the bookstore about being the perfect parent didn't even exist. If your kids were bad, you spanked 'em. Everyone did it. And you all turned out just fine."

This phenomenon, though, is a serious head-fuck. Just when our hormones start telling us that our bodies are irrelevant, many of us are also plagued by extreme emotional shifts or thoughts that have us wondering if we're losing it completely. Simultaneously, we live side-by-side with pimply-faced, hormone-driven creatures whose relevance is not to be questioned.

This is critical because it's easy to become so damn distracted that we don't notice our Prime Access programming coming to an end. By the time Christian had turned 13, I'd already had a 25-year career in marketing and branding, including owning an agency for almost 15 years. I didn't even realize that I'd reached a point where I could take it or leave it. I'd spent decades creating it, but I was *over* it.

Believe me, this isn't only true for women with kids. More women than ever before are choosing not to have kids. By the time they hit PrimeTime, they've invested themselves in careers that have spanned decades. Many of the PrimeTime women I worked with while creating this book were the most qualified they'd ever been and *filled* with potential. But they didn't see the transformations that were just around the corner.

Worse yet, many of the women I worked with saw the shifts coming, but believed that PrimeTime was already *over* for them. That 50 or 60 was the end of the big programming. They mistakenly believed they were already headed for the Late News daypart, which is only one hour long, and dedicated to reflections on what has *already occurred*.

So many of these women I surveyed were thinking about winding down careers, ending marriages, anticipating (or dreading) the day their kids would leave home. They were discussing issues like retirement and "settling down." When I asked them what they wanted to do next, many of them told me they planned to do nothing.

They had decided to just chill.

What the actual fuck?

The average life expectancy for a woman in America today is 81.3 years. This means that when my son graduates high school and leaves the house, I'll still have about 28 years of life left on this planet, if I'm average. (Which I am absolutely *not*. And neither are you.) We cannot spend three decades in the Late News daypart, for Christ's sake.

When I asked women approaching their 50s what their biggest questions or concerns were about getting older, the top four responses were:

1. What will I do with myself after my kids have left the house?
2. What will my husband/partner and I talk about when the kids are gone?
3. How can I keep my relationship interesting in the bedroom?
4. What will I do about my aging body?

If you're planning to chill for 30 years, I've got news for ya—that's not "doing something with yourself." It won't make you feel young. It won't promote fascinating conversations between you and your life partner. And it certainly won't make you sexier, more fit, or healthier.

But you know what will? Getting your actual groove on.

WHY WE'RE PERFECTLY PRIMED

"Middle-aged" is such a shitty term. While it may be chronologically accurate, it says nothing about the potential and capacity of the PrimeTime women I've met. They've worked in careers for 20 or 30 years. Or they've raised kids for decades. Many have done both. They've had long love relationships (or navigated a string of shorter ones) that were chock-full of lessons.

PrimeTime women are the wisest, most nimble creatures on Earth. They can juggle almost anything. They have stellar judgment. *They get it.*

If you had a real problem—I mean the kind that required strategy, quick reaction times, the possible use of duct tape, and absolute secrecy—who would you call?

A middle-aged man? HELL NO.

A woman in her 20s who's "relevant"? Fuck no.

If you need a job done right, you call a PrimeTime woman.

I will no longer stand by while we sell ourselves short and give ourselves away. Throughout the rest of this book, I'll teach you exactly what I've learned about how to do what you want during PrimeTime. What's more, I'll show you the ropes on how to do it without guilt, shame, explanation, or the need to blow up your life. So you can leap right out of bed every morning and say, "Today, I will *rock* this bitch!"

I'm also about to expose what's keeping you from doing that already. And why it's not your fault.

Do you know why we don't naturally rock PrimeTime? It's not because we're losers. It's not because we're weak. It's not because we're damaged or broken or "less motivated" than other, happier people. It's not even because we're tired. And contrary to what you might believe, it's not because we don't have time.

It's because we're bad at math, and we're liars.

Now before you go gettin' all indignant on me and telling me how you were accepted into the engineering program at MIT, I'm not talking about *that* kind of math. And I'm surely not saying that boys are better at math than girls. I have uncovered a widespread and destructive pattern in Prime-Time women that's grounded in completely common—but entirely flawed—answers to three math problems.

I've also discovered six ugly but pervasive lies that women tell themselves incessantly.

And to top it all off, I've identified a single question we should all be asking ourselves *first*, which simply never seems to come up.

One question. Three problems. Six lies. That's all that's standing between you and a PrimeTime show with ratings that are off the charts.

One question. Three problems. Six lies. On the other side of that, you're the star.

Are you with me?

CHAPTER 3

Mirror, Mirror, on the Wall

THE ONLY QUESTION THAT MATTERS

I'd bet dollars to donuts that if you and I met for cocktails and I asked you to tell me about yourself, you'd tell me instead about the roles that you fill. That's a trap that women our age find ourselves stuck in. By the time we've reached Prime-Time, we've spent our lives perfecting a list of roles as long as a line at the DMV.

At happy hour, you'd tell me about how you're a mom, a wife or partner, a daughter, an employee, a business owner, a volunteer, a friend, a sister, a lover, a domestic goddess, or a neighbor. These roles are awesome. And I have no doubt that you rock every single one.

We're super comfortable with our roles. But when it comes to our *essence*? Not so much.

Before we can cover the math and lies I mentioned earlier, I need to ask you one question that trumps every other question. For the purposes of this book, it is the only question that matters. But if you're like me and most other PrimeTime women, it's one you haven't asked yourself in quite a while:

What do you want?

I'm not looking for answers here like "I'll have the Kendall Jackson Chardonnay, please" or "All I want is a moment of peace" or "I'd love to have one of those Brazilian butt lifts like that girl down at the gym."

Tell me what you genuinely, passionately *want*.

I suspect the answer won't come easily. I've worked through this question with many different women, and even the strongest, most articulate, most successful women I coach give a long pause before answering.

Do you remember what life was like before you had kids? Before you were married? Before you were the PTA president or the Chairman of the Asset/Liability Committee at work? Before you adopted three dogs from the shelter or took out $50,000 in student loans that had to be repaid? Before you filled in every hour of your day with what you're *supposed* to do? Do you remember what your days were like before you committed yourself to everyone *else*? Back then, you knew what you wanted, and you went out and got it. Chasing pleasure was automatic, and you were rewarded with a big bunch of fun.

PrimeTime is about new beginnings. It's about creating passion around what you want, and being hell-bent on doing everything you possibly can to make it yours.

It's about the shit that stirs your soul.

WANTING WITH ABSOLUTE CLARITY

We have a 104-pound golden retriever named Diego. We used to tell ourselves he was just big-boned, but we've come to face the facts. He's fat. He has more junk in his trunk than a traveling encyclopedia salesman.

Don't get me wrong. Diego is gorgeous, in spite of his enormous ass. And we love him. But this dog can eat. And he does. Without regard to any other purpose in life. Because he is absolutely clear about what he *wants*, in every waking moment.

Before you go all judgey and shamey on me, like so many owners of lean dogs do, I promise you there's nothing *wrong* with Diego. We have the world's most attentive (and seemingly most expensive) veterinarian. She assures me that Diego's thyroid and other hormone levels, along with his vital signs and blood work, are all 100% normal. He's a healthy boy.

But he will not be dissuaded from what he wants.

Diego eats whole rolls of toilet paper. He once ate an entire rack of Costco ribs—bones, cellophane packaging, and all. He eats socks. He ate a slingshot. Not too long ago, he ingested a brand-new shower loofah.

Diego forages through our house for food as though he's lost in a dense, dark forest. Over the past eight years, he has snatched so many meals from Christian's plate that it's amazing our son has grown into a normal-sized young man. Diego shakes down every visitor who enters our home. Then he emotionally manipulates them for food—sometimes for hours on end—with practiced stares, sophisticated eyebrow movements, and expressions ranging from adorable to abused.

What I've learned from Diego is that when you are *absolutely clear* about what you want, a set of behaviors follows that ensures your success in obtaining it.

- Diego doesn't second-guess his mission; he's inspired by his vision of what *could* be.
- He never allows failed attempts to discourage him or wreak havoc on his self-esteem.
- He takes daily action with absolute consistency and unrestrained passion.
- He does not feel the need to apologize or provide explanation to anyone else.
- He believes that what he wants is naturally and rightfully his, and that he needn't do anything to *deserve* it.

I'll ask the question again.

What do you want?

THE QUESTION WE ASK INSTEAD

What most women are in touch with—often painfully—is the answer to a different question: What do I *not* want?

That's a start. It really is. But it only takes you part of the way there.

When I first launched my online course for women, I asked them what they wanted. And I honestly thought they would say, "I'd like to learn to ice skate" or "I'd love to speak Japanese" or "It's my dream to run a marathon." I was more than a little surprised when so many women told me first about what they *didn't* want. And that those things were so *big*.

Some women said they no longer wanted their marriages. Some said they wanted to trash their careers. Others no longer wanted to experience certain feelings, like the compulsion to pretend to be someone they weren't.

The PrimeTime women were most in touch with what they didn't want. And this is quite common. Once we hit peri-menopause and our hormones shift, our perspectives shift as well. Our roles related to caring for others come to an end. Our intuition strengthens. We become acutely aware of the unfinished business in our lives.

Contrary to what the world would say about PrimeTime women, we are anything *but* fragile. If you have relationships, responsibilities, habits, or activities in your life you don't want, you are not cracking up or falling apart. You are stronger and more resilient than you can imagine.

I trusted these women. So I asked them to dig deeper and answer the original question.

Because there are three problems with only knowing what you *don't* want.

First, tossing out what you don't want can sometimes leave a mighty big hole. And if you've got nothing to fill it up, you just might fall into it.

Second, sometimes the reason you don't want people, situations, routines, or even professions anymore is because you assumed that they would give you what you *do* want, and they're not performing properly. Maybe you think your marriage or your job or the size of your jeans is supposed to bring you happiness. Imagine, instead, how you'd feel about keeping stuff around if you had something for yourself that inspired you. Something you truly desired and pursued. Something that made you feel young again and new again and totally turned on. Would you still want to toss those "non-performing assets" into the dumpster?

Third, obsessing about what you don't want—without any focus on what you do want— can launch you into a horrible in-between state. We can't survive in limbo for too long. Limbo is an intermediate state. A state of neglect. Of oblivion. When you live in limbo, you put everything that matters on hold.

Passion? *Please hold.*

The glorious joy of beginning something exciting? *Not right now.*

Feelings of exhilaration? *Maybe later.*

Challenge, discovery, wonder, giddiness? *When it's time.*

If you could achieve joy and fulfillment through a process of elimination, you'd be all set. But total bliss requires some pursuit. If you think back to the last time you began again, you might remember that the pursuit is at least half the fun.

In order to make full use of this book—to create a PrimeTime where you bounce out of bed in the morning with a "Hot damn!" and an "I can't wait," you must ask yourself the only question that matters:

What do I want?

HEY, BEAUTIFUL. WHAT CAN I GET YA?

You may already know what you want. You may have known since you were 10. You may have been waiting to pursue it for the past 15 years, or shoved it deep down inside you because you convinced yourself that you'd never have it. If you're one of the lucky ones who knows what you want, then write it down when you've finished reading this chapter. You can write it right in this book. Or on an index card. Or on your hand. Or any place you want. But finish the chapter, because you need to know the rules.

Now, if you have no idea what you want, then you should know you're among friends. Enough friends to fill a stadium. You should also learn a rather fun way to figure it out. That is, if you're willing to feel a bit silly, and stick with it until you find your answer.

EXERCISE: "HEY, GORGEOUS."

Louise Hay has a beautiful practice that she calls "mirror work." It's super powerful, and it produces real results where self-love and acceptance are concerned. I've modified it, though, (on the advice of a remarkable coach and friend of mine named Yara Golden), to support the inquiry around what your heart and soul desire.

Every morning, before you run off to fill a role that's wrapped around what someone else needs or what the whole world wants from you, spend 10 or 15 minutes with yourself in front of the mirror.

First, you'll need to LOOK at yourself in the mirror. Look deep into your eyes. Hold your gaze. Do not let go. And smile, for God's sake. Right at your beautiful self.

For this exercise, you'll need to give yourself a pet name. I call myself Gorgeous. As in, "Hey, Gorgeous. What's your name? You lookin' for some action?"

In Louise Hay's version of mirror work, you tell yourself one critical statement, over and over, each day: "Life loves you." There's an important catch to this statement. Life doesn't love you *because* of anything. You don't need to earn it. You aren't supposed to try for it. You don't have to deserve it. It's just a truth. Life loves you. The universe has your back.

So you look in the mirror and say, "Hey, Gorgeous. Life loves you." Say it 15 times.

This is gonna feel weird. You'll probably feel uncomfortable. You might even find it ridiculous. But it's a game changer. It's a hothouse for dream-growers.

Now here's the clincher. After you tell yourself that life loves you, ask yourself:

"What do I want?"

The answer won't come the first day. It might not even come on the tenth day. But it will come. It will most definitely come, if you stick with it.

Here's why the "Life loves you" part is so important. By beginning first with this absolute truth—by understanding that you are loved and you are supported—you will make it safe for whatever you want to enter your life.

The exercise is this super straightforward.

1. Hello, Gorgeous.
2. (Give yourself a radiant smile.)
3. Life loves you.
4. What do you want?

Talk to yourself the way you'd talk to anyone who benefits from the roles you fill. If your best friend was floundering, how would you ask her what she wants? If your child had a fever, and you wanted to soothe them, how would you ask? If your boss was working toward a deadline, and you wanted to be helpful and productive, how would you ask her what she wants?

THE RULES FOR WHAT YOU WANT

There are rules to this game, and if you break them, you'll screw it all up for yourself. I'm asking you to trust me, and follow them completely.

- Do NOT put limitations or restrictions on what you want.

- Do NOT provide reasons for why you don't yet have what you want.

- Do NOT consider whether you deserve what you want.

- Do NOT, in any way, judge what you want.

- Do NOT make excuses for wanting what you want.

You've spent your whole life asking other people what THEY want.

Just ask yourself the fucking question until the answer shows up.

"Hi, Gorgeous. Life loves you. What do you want?"

Then write it down.

When you're finished, we can start the math lessons.

PART II

The Three Problems

CHAPTER 4

Mad Girl Math

THE NAME OF THE GAME

When our son, Christian, was in the third grade, he embarked on a long-term challenge called Mad Dog Math. The idea was that eight-year-olds, during a time when their brains were especially spongy, should soak up *math facts* through repetition and speed. These facts would provide the solid foundation upon which they would build a lifetime of complex problem-solving skills. By the time the challenge was completed, the members of this mathtastic little army knew the answer to 7 × 9 as well as they knew their own names.

Mad Dog Math featured a test every day. One number, multiplied by 1 through 12, both backward and forward, for a total of 24 problems. The tests in the first round were two minutes long. If Christian completed all 24 problems in less than two minutes and got fewer than two wrong, on the following day he could advance to the test for the next number. If not—like a mad dog—he kept at it until he got what he was after. Then came a round of 1-minute tests, and after that, 30-second tests. Every kid in the class was at a different place in the game on the same day, resulting in a kind of controlled mayhem.

Mad Dog Math was all-consuming, and it produced a mad mom, a mad dad, and one colossally mad Christmas vacation. It also set Christian up with a series of equations, the answers to which he came to adopt as absolute truth.

PrimeTime women also play a kind of math game. I call it Mad Girl Math. It involves only three problems, and we have practiced them so long and so hard that we've come to believe our answers are the absolute truth. But it's different than Mad Dog Math, because our answers are not mathematically proven.

In fact, they are 100% false. They are illogical. They are bad math. They are bullshit. And what they produce is a foundation upon which we build a solid and enduring practice of failing to make significant changes in our lives, and refusing to seek what we truly desire.

Before I reveal the three problems, let me explain what I mean by Mad Girl, because several definitions of *mad* appear in the dictionary. And each and every one applies here.

- First, mad means insane. This definition applies, because it's easy to question our own mental health when we're in the state created by these problems.

- Second, mad means angry. Mad Girl Math pisses us off and frustrates us. It makes us feel wronged and put out. It is the basis for so much moral outrage.

- And third, mad has a slang usage meaning "a lot" or "extreme." When used properly in a sentence, it sounds like: "She's got mad misconceptions about life, dude." Or "That girl's got mad problems when it comes to takin' care of her shit."

Don't make me define *girl*. I don't care how old you are. You're my girl.

Mad Girl Math is based entirely on three equations that are entirely erroneous, yet we overwhelmingly *believe* to be correct. Over time, accepting these equations will kill your dreams, your motivation, your relationships, your self-esteem, and most definitely any chance you have at a Prime-Time that sets your panties on fire.

Imagine for a moment that you grew up believing that 3 × 3 = 10. What would happen when you approached a problem like 10 ÷ 2 and tried to arrive at an answer that made sense in real life? You'd be screwed. What if you computed 3 × 4? Screwed again. Think about when you were faced with the complicated or tedious shit, like long division or fractions! You would be thrust into a world of ridiculous hurt.

The same is true with Mad Girl Math. When we take these equations as the basis for fact, every calculation we make in life beyond them is flawed. Which means that even if I show you the truth after you make the mistake, you won't believe it. Because it won't make any sense to you.

In the chapters that follow, I'll break down each one of these equations and show you just how faulty they are, and how they play out in our daily lives.

THE WRONG KIND OF QUESTION

But first, let's talk for just a quick moment about *why*.

Why do we buy into this Mad Girl Math? Why do we function, essentially, on a mountain of faulty premises? It could be social programming. Maybe it's the way our parents raised us or how we learned to attract attention or work our way out of trouble. Mad Girl Math could be part of our religious background, or born from behaviors that were modeled for us by leaders or mentors. It could be a function of pervasive cultural bias, or even a conspiracy against us. I am absolutely certain that women way smarter and more experienced than me can answer the "why" question with startling historical and psychological data and context.

The truth is, though, I don't care why. And you shouldn't either. "Why" is irrelevant for our purposes here. It's simply not helpful.

As a general rule, questions that begin with "why" facilitate a look *backward*. They are used to understand the past. Furthermore, our brain tends to answer "why" questions in a rather dark way. We end up chasing answers that will never serve us. And we chase them right down into rabbit holes. My own beautiful and exceptionally wise coach, Mandy, told me that unless I'm wearing a white lab coat and conducting an experiment using the scientific method, "why" questions are basically bullshit.

This book is about moving forward into PrimeTime. It's about pursuing what you want. So rather than asking "why" questions, I'd love for you to ask these:

- Who?
- What?
- How?

The answers to those kinds of questions will lead you right where you want to go, baby.

Now, let's get back to that math.

CHAPTER 5

My Thoughts = X

PRINCESS MOMO CALLS ME OUT

My friend Johanna's mom is named Sandia. She's a 78-year-old hippie who wears Chuck Taylor All Stars, hand-woven Alpaca ponchos, and the occasional Nehru jacket. She never misses a local gay pride march, posts the best memes on Facebook, and flirts like a champion. She's also a laugh a fucking minute.

When Johanna's son was born, Sandia didn't want to be called Grandma. She preferred to be called Princess Momo. So now we all call her Momo, for short.

Momo is a life-long meditator. She lives half of every year in a monastery in India, where she helps care for orphan kids. As a general rule, Momo pursues an almost scandalous level of personal happiness that she feels zero need to apologize for.

About 10 years ago, a bunch of our friends had lunch with her at our favorite little Peruvian restaurant, on the day she returned home from an ashram. She had spent seven straight days in silent meditation. For more than 100 hours she sat quietly, and simply watched her thoughts march by like an electric light parade.

We're a pretty yappy group, and we were all stunned by Momo's desire to complete such a seemingly nutty undertaking. Our friend Artie finally asked her the question that was on everyone's lips. "Momo, did you learn anything?"

She took a long pull off her bottle of Negro Modelo and replied, "Yes. I learned that thong underwear is not the best choice for seven days in the lotus position."

Momo had sat for seven days, watching her thoughts, without entertaining a single one. Her primary mission was to ignore them completely. I was aghast.

For as long as I could remember, I'd been a victim of my thoughts. I believed they controlled me. I was haunted by them. Validated by them. Tortured by them. Led around by them. Compelled to share them with anyone who would listen. I was sure they were ethereal representations of absolute reality. On days when my thoughts were shitty, I believed I was shitty, my friends were shitty, and my life was shitty. On days when my thoughts were brilliant, the sun shone out of my ass.

It was Momo who introduced me to the first math problem. She showed me that the Mad Girl version of the equation looks like this:

MY THOUGHTS = REALITY

She also taught me the brutal truth. That the correct answer to the equation is this:

MY THOUGHTS = BULLSHIT

I had several conversations with Momo after that day at the Peruvian restaurant, and I tried to believe her about the bullshit. But I couldn't take her at face value. That just seemed irresponsible. So I read about 65 books on meditation.

Then one day, as I cried to her in complete and utter confusion, she said, "Juju, you don't need to read anything else. Just start meditating."

I knew she was right; I just didn't think I was qualified to go it alone. And in that moment, I decided to go on my own brave journey. But because the beds at the ashram sounded awfully hard and the required silence was a deal-breaker for me, I chose the next best thing: a week at the La Costa Spa and Resort with Deepak Chopra.

I had already read every one of Deepak's books, and I proudly considered myself a bit of a New Ager. My husband thought I needed a little less Deepak and a little more Tupac. But in the end, he relented, and paid several thousand dollars so I could have a celebrity guru teach me how not to think.

Jan assumed that for the price he'd paid, Deepak and I and a couple other searchers would be sitting on a mat somewhere together, bonding. When I called home and told him 400 people were sitting in lotus position in the Poinsettia Ballroom, he said, "What the fuck? This guy makes more money than Mick Jagger."

My week at La Costa, as pithy as it may sound, profoundly changed me. When I came home, Jan said, "I don't know what happened to you, but I hope it keeps happening." Christian, who was five at the time, asked if he could "levitate" with me. Even he saw the change, and he wanted some of what I had.

I didn't stop with Deepak. I spent the next four years validating that I was, indeed, entirely full of shit. I read everything from Ram Dass to texts on quantum physics to Steve Martin. I took up yoga and eventually got my 200-hour teaching certification in the Ashtanga method. I made Tibetan bowls sing and chanted to Hanuman. I became a vegan and ate so much pasta that I gained 30 pounds. I attended a breath-work session where I hyperventilated and cried my eyes out. I enjoyed a massage by a Reiki master and hallucinated that I was traveling through a tunnel of color. I studied comparative religion like a fiend.

And I became ridiculously, deliriously happy.

Every single bit of it hinged on one equation that I relearned, again and again:

MY THOUGHTS ≠ REALITY

MY THOUGHTS = BULLSHIT

You may decide to go on your own journey. Or you may decide just to read this book and go for margaritas. Either way, I'll break down the basics for you. Because if you plan to crush it in PrimeTime, you need to understand this equation inside and out.

HAS IT EVER OCCURRED TO YOU?

Simply speaking, you can't believe everything you think. This is a hard pill to swallow, because our thoughts are incessant. We have conversations with ourselves day in and day out, our whole lives.

On average, we have between 50,000 and 70,000 thoughts per day. That's between 35 and 48 thoughts per minute. It's entirely natural to feel like what's happening in our heads— this barrage of reaction, analysis, assessment, prediction, judgment, and imagining—represents reality. But nothing could be further from the truth. When you begin to see your thoughts for what they truly are, you free yourself up for the glorious pursuit of what you truly want.

For starters, you should realize that thinking is a spectator sport. And I've got news for you. You are the spectator, not one of the boxers in the ring. You are the one in the stands. This is easy to prove to yourself. Just wait for your next thought. Hear it. See it. And realize that you are the one doing the one watching. *You are not your thoughts.* You are the one witnessing them.

Now let's break down where thoughts come from. We believe—and live by—the notion that our thoughts come from within us. But that's a misconception. Your thoughts don't come *from* you. They come *to* you. "That just occurred to me" is part of our vernacular for a reason.

Your thoughts are occurrences. They're happenings. They're instances. They're phenomena. Like lightning. Or the doorbell ringing. Or that sound the mustard bottle makes if you forget to shake it. They are nothing more than occurrences.

Now this next part is even *more* of a mind-blower. Your thoughts occur *only* to *you*. You are the only one in the stands watching this particular boxing match. Outside of your head, your thoughts have zero reality. No substance, no power, no influence, no impact. They simply do not exist outside of you.

I had a seriously hard time with this concept until I heard Deepak Chopra's delightfully easy-to-understand, albeit graphic, explanation. He said that if we cleaved our heads open, we would never find a repository for our thoughts. There would be no hard drives with megabytes of our thoughts stored on them. No piles of thoughts would tumble out. We would find no place in our brains where thoughts were filed away in folders. They simply wouldn't be there. Because they have no substance. They are not real. And they come from outside us.

Here's an even more powerful way to look at this. If you have a thought, and you don't give it any attention—if you don't wrap a bunch of judgey stuff around it and build a story—it will simply disappear. It will come... and it will go. And literally NOTHING will have happened as a result. Zero. Nada.

But we don't do that, do we? Instead, we *entertain* our thoughts and ideas. They drop by without calling first, and we *entertain* them. We let them in, and give them a nice place to hang out, raid the fridge, lie on the couch, and bug the shit out of us—so that they *become* reality. They're like our husband's fat, lazy college roommate who moves in with us and refuses to look for a job.

Our thoughts *are not* matter. And they *do not* matter. We *make* them matter.

Let me give you an example. Let's say that your best friend, Alicia, meets a new friend, Ruby, at the office, and they go out for happy hour. Without you. And you start to have thoughts, like this:

> *Alicia is rude. She should have invited me. She knows she hurt my feelings, but she doesn't care. Ruby is probably fascinating. I bet she has great hair and skydives and is super funny. Alicia will probably dump me for Ruby, and I'll be stuck drinking alone. Our relationship is falling apart.*

Let's break this down, using our new knowledge that MY THOUGHTS = BULLSHIT.

- You are not this thought. You are watching this thought.
- This thought did not come from you. It came to you. It *occurred to you* that what Alicia did was hurtful. You are not obligated to believe it. You are not required to attend every thought party to which you're invited. The thought has no power over you.
- That thought has no existence outside of your head. Just because you think Alicia is insensitive doesn't mean that she truly is. Furthermore, Alicia has no idea

what you are thinking. She cannot read your mind. (And frankly, if this is the kind of shit that's rolling around in there, she's lucky she can't.)

- If I chopped your head open, this thought would not fall out. It has no substance. It has no reality.

- If you give the thought zero attention—if you refuse to fuel it with intention or interest or emotion—the thought will, eventually, just disappear. It will be there and it will be gone. Nothing will have changed because you had the thought.

- But if you entertain the thought, it will hang around. It will frustrate you and torture you and turn you into a nutjob. If you let it lie on the couch, it will suck the life out of your headspace.

Then…you will do something about the thought. You will make it real. You will manifest it into actual existence. You will say something nasty to Alicia. Or sabotage your friendship in a passive-aggressive way. Or skip your yoga class and lie around sulking. Or tell your husband what a bitch Alicia is. Or refuse to meet Ruby when Alicia invites you to, and miss out on a new friend.

You have the power to simply watch the thought come and watch the thought go. You have the power to give it no power. But once you act on it, you make it real.

How neat is *that*?

MY THOUGHTS ≠ REALITY

MY THOUGHTS = BULLSHIT

Why is this important? Because in the last chapter, I asked you to identify what you *want*. And do you know what your thoughts will do to what you want? They will crucify it.

If you entertain the thoughts that occur to you about your big, scary PrimeTime endeavor, you will convince yourself that your dreams are wrong. That you can never have them. That life is too hard, that too many roadblocks stand in your way, that your pursuit will never succeed, that your kids are secretly working to sabotage you, that your spouse doesn't sincerely want what's best for you, or that life should be fair. Your thoughts might just tell you that you're too stupid or too much of a loser to go out and do what you've always wanted to do.

You know what action you'll take? You'll quit. Or, like me, you'll never even begin. You'll never give yourself a chance at all.

GET OUTTA THERE

One of the world's foremost experts on self-esteem is Nathaniel Branden. In an article he wrote called "What Self-Esteem Is, and What It Is Not" he says:

> When we seek to align ourselves with reality as best we understand it, we nurture and support our self-esteem. When, either out of fear or desire, we seek escape from reality, we undermine our self-esteem. No other issue is more important or basic than our cognitive relationship to reality—meaning: to that which exists.

While the book you're reading right now isn't necessarily about self-esteem, it is about knowing you deserve what you desire. And in order to grab what's yours, you must have courage, resilience, the ability to see clearly what's required to obtain it, and a belief that you can do it. You'll also need to have a nice, healthy relationship with reality.

And you'll need to get out of your head.

So if MY THOUGHTS ≠ REALITY, then what the fuck is reality? As Branden so clearly and simply states, REALITY = THAT WHICH EXISTS.

This all sounds pretty woo-woo, I know. And you may be wondering why I'm taking you down a path that sounds like it should be fragrant with incense and chiming with tinkly bells. But I promise you, it's relevant to the PrimeTime show that is about to become your life.

As you move forward in PrimeTime, you will be plagued by thoughts. The part of you that you're booting out—the part of you that would never pursue such a gutsy and fantastic goal—is not going to take this lying down. She will fight back from inside your mind. She will cry out and tell you all kinds of horribly untrue bullshit to convince you to quit as soon as your new endeavors become the slightest bit difficult. You must remember that she is not real. She has no power over you. But she's a trained professional.

If you want to beat her, you'd be awfully wise to practice. The same way you'd practice the trombone or Kegel exercises or applying the perfect lip liner.

I strongly suggest that you adopt two effortless and utterly delightful practices:

- MEDITATION: watching your thoughts
- MINDFULNESS: becoming aware of that which exists in any given moment

Taken together, these two practices will bring you more happiness and more strength than you can possibly imagine. The benefits are untold. These two practices will let you glide through PrimeTime without the embarrassing (and often downright dangerous) incidents that could arise if you let the voice in your head drive the car.

What I hear most often when I coach people through this is "Juju, I cannot meditate. I cannot stop my thoughts." That is 100% correct. As my brother, Tom, would have said, "You bet your sweet bippy, you can't." But the best part is, you don't even need to try.

Instead, you just need to practice observing your thoughts, recognizing that they are not reality, and becoming crystal clear about what reality is. Period. These practices are not difficult. They require no effort. In fact, if you have to try, you're doing it wrong.

MEDITATION

Why should you meditate? To practice being a spectator. To recognize that your thoughts are not reality. And to become comfortable with letting them pass, without entertaining them or acting on them.

The most straightforward and easily adoptable approach to meditation I've ever seen is in Deepak Chopra's book, *Perfect Health, The Complete Mind and Body Guide.* You can begin today. It requires no trips to the La Costa Resort, no investment of thousands of dollars, and no hard ashram beds. You do not need to wear special pants, rub coconut oil on yourself, or purchase a pillow or mat. If you would like to facilitate any of those experiences, knock yourself out. But if not, just do what I say.

1. Find a quiet place to sit, and close your eyes. You can lie down if you must, but sitting up is preferable, because it's easy to fall asleep otherwise.

2. Take a couple of deep breaths. Fill your chest and your belly. And exhale forcefully.

3. Begin to breathe normally. Bring your attention to your breath.

4. Each time you inhale, silently say to yourself, "SO."

5. Each time you exhale, silently say to yourself, "HUM."

6. Focus on your breath and the words.

7. Do not try to breathe any certain way. Just let your breath flow naturally.

8. When a thought comes up, notice it, and return to your SO/HUM.

9. Don't scold yourself about the thought. Don't wrap a story around the thought.

10. Just return gently to SO/HUM.

That's it. That's meditating.

People say to me, "Juju, that sounds incredibly boring." But it's surprisingly pleasant, if you do it as instructed. You don't need to meditate for an hour, or for seven days straight. You can meditate for 5 or 10 minutes a day to begin with. If you're the type who likes structure, set an alarm on your phone.

Learn to take serious comfort in this solution: MY THOUGHTS = BULLSHIT.

MINDFULNESS

Why should you practice mindfulness? Because, if your thoughts are not reality, it's essential to know what is. In addition to that, it will make you feel super groovy. It will calm your shit down, generally make you more grateful and less reactive to the little stuff that would ordinarily piss you off, and make your day much sunnier. Mindfulness is the bee's knees. And, like meditation, it has zero degree of difficulty and requires zero effort.

1. Choose a task that you do daily, like laundry or dishes, putting on your make-up, or making your lunch. To begin, pick something that takes only a few minutes.

2. Until you get the hang of it (and want to possibly explore other kinds of practices), use the same task

every day. That will allow you to be "in flow" more quickly.

3. Now elevate this task to an experience.

4. As you are completing the task, focus your attention entirely on each step.

5. Pay attention to what you are touching and what it feels like.

6. Take note of what you are hearing and what it sounds like.

7. Focus on smells and sights and the smallest of details.

8. If your mind begins to wander or you have thoughts outside of the task, gently return your attention to the task at hand.

9. Fully immerse yourself in this process and see reality.

10. Do this practice every day.

Can you see where I'm going with this? Your power, your presence, your ability to commit, your willingness to see your potential clearly will come from knowing the difference between bullshit and reality. And while this sounds like "Being Human 101," this is not the natural state for women in PrimeTime. We are busy. We are distracted. We are stuck in our ways. We are not used to opening ourselves up to new ways of life.

If you want to nail everlasting happiness and PrimeTime success, find a way to observe your thoughts and a way to connect with reality. If you don't like the practices I've provided here, just google this shit. You'll find about 15,000 alternatives.

But get your head on straight.

MY THOUGHTS ≠ REALITY

MY THOUGHTS = BULLSHIT

Now that we've covered your thoughts, let's talk about your feelings. And the next Mad Girl Math problem.

CHAPTER 6

My Emotions = X

ARE YA FEELIN' ME?

I met my current husband, Jan, when I was 30. I had recently left a husband whom I'd been married to for 10 years to marry another man whom I had no idea was gay. (Go ahead. Try and wrap your head around that one.) Shit was complicated, and I was more than a little unhinged. I hated my executive job. I dragged my ass to work every day as an uncommitted leader stuck inside the hell of her own mind.

My mental health was sketchy at best, and I was still light years away from understanding that MY THOUGHTS = BULLSHIT. I had a bottle of anti-depressants and twice-weekly sessions with a therapist named Andrea. I'm sure if anyone had asked her, she'd have told them that this shit was way above her paygrade.

Then one day, out of the blue, a German superhero showed up at the office. He was 25, was working on his thesis for a double degree in macro-economics and international management, and had decided to complete a summer banking internship in America.

Jan was gorgeous: 6'2", blond hair that hung past his shoulders, perfectly tailored three-piece Hugo Boss suit, and a wide, easy smile that knocked me straight onto my ass. The ladies in the phone center at work called him Fabio. He was captivated by the Southern California surf culture, and spent every morning before work and every evening after trying to catch a wave. He was the best paddler on the beach.

He was also whip-smart and wise to the world in a way I had never been. He had grown up behind the Berlin Wall. At the age of 17, he'd been convinced by Western culture that everything he'd believed in was wrong, and the shifts that occurred in his society, his family, his friendships, and his future made him both a heady philosopher and an angry pragmatist. I found him fascinating. I literally could not get enough of him.

For the first time in my life, I experienced the *feeling* of mad, passionate love. I felt the sickness in my stomach. The sweat in my palms. The beating of my heart. The flush in my cheeks. I was plagued by every ridiculously clichéd physiological reaction that's ever been linked to love. I fell hard. And the nasty thoughts in my head that had ruled the roost since I was a teen were immediately and summarily kicked to the curb. My feelings took the wheel. And they took me for a dangerously wild ride.

Jan will tell you that he didn't fall in love until about 18 months later, once he verified that I wasn't certifiably insane. But I know now that he's rewritten history. He had it for me, too. The electricity was incredible. From the moment we met on the first of July, we spent every possible free hour together.

At the same time, we made the conscious choice to call what we had a "summer fling." A long-distance romance between Newport Beach and Berlin seemed unreasonable by any standard. So we made pacts. Like "I really care about you, but when this is over, it's over. In October, we're done." And "I don't love you. I won't say that I do. So let's agree not to go there." The relationship was ludicrous, on every level. But seriously hot.

We spent every day of that summer falling in love. As October drew near, we both admitted what we'd been afraid to say. The agreements flew out the window, and we decided that breaking up seemed more absurd than staying together. 'Round about that time, the executive management team I was a part of decided that my decision to date the summer intern was irresponsible, at best. And I walked away from a six-figure job—broken and shamed, but wildly, madly in love. Life was a fucking circus.

Then he got on a plane, and he left.

I retreated to my older brother's house in Yuma, Arizona, where I licked my wounds, and got a part-time job as a DJ on the local classic rock station. I called myself Jewel in the Desert. My brother and his wife doubted that Jan was an actual person, and did their best to accommodate what appeared to be a psychotic break on my part, instigated by a monumental life change that had culminated in my job loss.

From the moment Jan walked out my door in California until the moment I walked through his door in Berlin 90 days later, I was ruled by emotional whiplash. The trauma was caused by my undying belief in the second of the Mad Girl Math equations:

MY FEELINGS = FACTS

Pretty much every day went something like this:

Before bed, I would write Jan a 1,000-word email about how much I missed him and couldn't wait to see him. The message would also include a detailed account of my day. Jan was a man of few words. And at the time, those words came much more naturally to him in German than in English. In addition to that, he actually had a life. So he responded to my missives with short little quips like "Ok" or "Love you, baby."

I would wake in the morning, rush to my computer, find his trivial response, and set into motion a vicious and wholly unnecessary physiological cycle. Because I didn't realize that MY THOUGHTS = BULLSHIT, I entertained them with raucous parties. The noise from my riotous frontal cortex alerted my hypothalamus, which reacted by altering my heart rate, blood pressure, breathing rate, stress levels, and hormone secretion.

My lover had not responded to my message in kind, so danger was imminent!

Our thoughts might equal bullshit, my friend, but our feelings are very, very real.

What they are NOT is factual.

Something interesting happens when we equate our feelings to facts. We eliminate the need to verify our conclusions. We assume that because what we feel is *real*, it is also *true*. We blindly follow these non-truths. And when we do, we give up amazing amounts of power. And we put into danger our goals, desires, and passions.

Each day as I waited for Jan to call, I followed my feelings as fact. At breakfast, the lump in my throat and the heaviness in my chest would convince me that Jan didn't love me. It had all been a sham. Crushed and defeated, I would call myself foolish and a loser. By lunch, when the phone had still refused to ring, I would allow the constricted feeling in my gut, my total loss of appetite, and my rapid heart rate to convince me that Jan was with another girl. I needed to protect myself. Angry and defensive, I would march through the afternoon, cursing at him in my mind. By dinner, the flush in my face would convince me that he was a liar. He had taken me for a ride, and he was a monster. I was a victim. The struggle was real.

But then the phone would ring. I would hear his voice. He would tell me that he loved me. We would talk about our days. The sweaty palms and the flutters in my stomach and the warm feeling all over would return. And I'd head to bed to rest up for the next day, when once again I would be chased through the woods by a bear from sunrise to sunset.

My best friend, Stacy, told me during this time that I was the only person she knew who could have a fight with someone—complete with swearing, accusations, crying, pathetic excuses, eventual truth, and full-blown make-up sex—all without ever having spoken to him. I knew she was right. But I know now that she was wrong about me being the only one. MY FEEL-INGS = FACTS is the foundation of many a woman's misery. For PrimeTime women, it can be especially debilitating.

YOU'VE LOST THAT LOVING FEELING

Why is this equation so important in PrimeTime? Because, my friend, PrimeTime is GO TIME when it comes to emotions. It's the Big Top, baby. It's the Kentucky Derby. It's the World Cup. There are three reasons we need to be completely square with the truth at this point in our lives.

First, menopause is a bona fide phenomenon. Around age 35, when our hormones begin to decline, the hormone receptors in our body—the ones accustomed to receiving estrogen and progesterone—begin to starve. This is the beginning of perimenopause. Many of those receptors are in our brains. What results from this starvation is a wonky chain of biochemical activity that ultimately affects our mood-regulating chemicals, including serotonin and endorphins. Add to that the fact that altered estrogen levels affect both our quantity and quality of sleep, and you've got a recipe for mayhem.

We can swing from furious to despondent to exasperated to elated in a matter of hours. Now pile on the hormonal changes that your teenagers are going through at the same time…and you've got yourself a "holy cow" situation.

For some reason, we're conditioned to believe that this is a sign of weakness. And I know a ton of women who want to pretend it's not happening. Instead of admitting that their hormones have up-ended their senses, they try to defend their emotions. They feel the need to bring reason to the madness. They lean on the equation MY FEELINGS = FACTS so they don't appear to be crazy. This, in turn, makes everyone around them crazy instead.

Second, and even more confusing, is the fact that changes in our temporal lobes give us access to enhanced intuition during this time in our lives. Which means that if situations in your life that need to be changed—ones you've been putting off, living with, or sweeping under the rug—you may be more aware of them during PrimeTime. Because one of the hallmarks of PrimeTime is transition—kids are leaving the house, retirement is near, our parents may be reaching an age where they need constant care—a whole lot of shit can come up that we've kept at bay for quite a long time.

When I was in my mid-30s, I had a business colleague named Claudia. She had succumbed fully to the ebb and flow of her menopausal emotions, and linked them squarely to fact. She told me she had come to hate her husband. She couldn't stand the sound of his voice. She even dreamt of killing him. She couldn't wait to find a way to ditch him. It had finally occurred to her, from one day to the next, that he was a colossal asshole who deserved to be tossed over a bridge, with cement blocks tied to his feet. In every moment, her feelings informed her thoughts, and her thoughts reinforced her feelings. She was so deep into it that she couldn't tell a fact from a french fry. And her certainty scared the shit out of me.

But there's a third reason, beyond menopause, that understanding this equation is so critical at this juncture in our lives. Because if we want to make PrimeTime the best time, we'll need to muster courage. We'll take risks, buck the system, wage against the status quo, and make some changes in our lives. This may bring up some devastatingly strong feelings. If we mistake our feelings for facts, we'll never be able to push through. With every swing of the emotional pendulum, we'll convince ourselves that what we want is foolish. That our chance at achieving it is nil. And that our right to have it is constantly in question.

Now more than ever, we need the right answer to the equation.

JUST THE FACTS, MA'AM

Facts exist outside of us. They can be proven through data, through objective analysis, or through scientific verification.

Our feelings exist inside of us. They are real. They are visceral. They are happening. And they are, quite simply, *reactions to stimuli*. That's the truth of the equation, right there.

MY FEELINGS ≠ FACTS
MY FEELINGS = REACTIONS TO STIMULI

Sometimes, that stimulus comes from outside of us. We react to an occurrence, to something someone said, to the weather, to a TV show, to a song we hear on the radio, to the sound of a child crying. Or as my mom used to say, to a "lippy, smart-aleck" teenager.

Sometimes, that stimulus comes from inside of us. We react to shifts in our hormones, alcohol or drugs we've ingested, blood sugar levels, sleep deprivation, and an entire host of bodily functions.

At other times, those stimuli are our *thoughts*. Our limbic system reacts when our frontal cortex engages. Our mind informs our body.

Our feelings are real. But they are not facts. They are reactions.

The fact that many of your PrimeTime feelings are reactions to menopausal hormone shifts should be an amazing relief. It's a Get Out of Jail Free card. It gives you a legitimate and medically proven reason for feeling the way you feel. As long as you remember the #1 rule associated with this equation:

> You may not be responsible for the stimulus that incited an emotion, but you are *always* responsible for the actions you take in response to that emotion.

Much like our thoughts, we can entertain our feelings, stoke them, wallow in them, and use them as weapons. Likewise, we can bury them. Refuse to feel them. We fuel addictions and self-sabotaging behaviors in order to avoid them. Or blame them on the people around us.

The trick to working the MY FEELINGS = REACTIONS TO STIMULI equation is to *allow* yourself to feel something, then put some time and space between the feeling and any action you might take as a result.

When my son was a toddler, I used to count to 10. When I turned 50, 10 was not nearly enough. You need time and space to reflect. To be aware of what you're feeling and aware of what triggered it.

MULTIPLE EQUATIONS

One of the most effective ways I've been trained to regulate my own negative emotions and coached others to regulate theirs is to remember the first Mad Girl Math equation. MY THOUGHTS = BULLSHIT. Regulating negative emotions allows us to reduce the potential pain that comes from sitting inside them.

And what's incredibly powerful, in addition to calling out our Mad Girl Math, is a practice that therapists call cognitive reappraisal. Byron Katie, in her book *Loving What Is*, calls her similar and amazing system The Work. In strategic planning, we called this What-If Analysis. KellyAnne Conway calls it alternative facts. Whatever you call it, it's all rooted in fantasy. Yet it works like an absolute charm.

Based on what you learned in the last chapter, you're already a pro at watching your thoughts. But in this case, you won't just be observing passively. You'll be looking for patterns.

When your emotions spin out of control, a negative feedback loop begins to operate. Your emotions feed your thoughts, which feed your emotions, which feed your thoughts. If you can ease into the spectator seat and watch the thoughts float by, you can watch yourself "appraising" the situation. You provide commentary and analysis regarding the situation (the stimulus). In your mind, you assign meaning to it.

When you're in the spectator seat, you'll recognize that this is not fact; it's all based on mood, speculation, and imaginings of what could happen. Here's the clincher: In the same way that you created the first pattern of appraisals you witnessed, you could just as easily consider an *alternative* set of appraisals. Or a whole ton of alternatives. And taking a moment to do this will shift your mood, help alleviate the pain, and give you some space and time, so you can avoid taking action you might regret.

Let's consider the emotional merry-go-round I rode during my long-distance relationship with Jan. When I woke up in the morning to his non-responsive replies to my emails (the stimuli), I reacted with a feeling. That feeling led to an appraisal of the situation. Which further fed the feeling. And soon, those appraisals turned into a pattern.

- *He hates my emails.*
- *I always talk more than I should. I'm such a loser.*

- *He doesn't want to talk to me. He's over me.*
- *He didn't have time to answer because he was out with someone else.*

None of those appraisals was based on fact. What's more, because they were nothing more than evaluations of a situation based on fantasy and conjecture, an infinite number of *alternate* evaluations (or reappraisals) could have also been taken into account. Fantasy is fantasy, right?

Consider these alternatives:

- *He had a soccer game last night. He was probably exhausted.*
- *He hates writing in English. But I'm sure he loves reading my stuff.*
- *He's a guy, and therefore uncomfortable with this kind of stuff.*
- *He must be super busy.*

If you can recognize the pattern of your appraisals—if you can see how you're using non-facts to interpret the stimuli that caused your feeling—you can reappraise. And save yourself from yourself.

If you suspect that I am irrational and you are not—and therefore that this doesn't apply to you—let me show you how reappraisal works in a fairly mundane but common situation during PrimeTime. Because we all appraise. We all guess. We all speculate. We all predict the future. And we all judge. It's basic human nature.

As research for this book, I talked to as many women over 40 as I could find. I also talked to some of the teens who were being raised by them. I made it my business to open up this line of discussion everywhere I went.

One Saturday morning, I met a smart and totally captivating teenage girl who was bagging my groceries at Trader Joe's. I got to talking with the cashier about menopausal moms raising teens, and there was an audible groan from the young lady.

"What's that?" I asked. "Have you been through this?"

"Oh, yeah," she said. "My mom and I used to have the BEST relationship. Until she started flipping her lid over things like how I put the vacuum cleaner away. She went totally nuts if I didn't wind up the cord."

So let's work some cognitive appraisal on this situation, shall we?

Maggie has put the vacuum cleaner away without winding up the cord. Mom has told Maggie a thousand times that proper cord-winding is key to long-term vacuum success. Following are some appraisals of the situation that might naturally come to Mom's mind:

- *Maggie never listens to me. I speak and she completely ignores me.*
- *Maggie is totally disrespectful. She knows this shit makes me crazy, but she does it anyway!*
- *Maggie will never make it in life because she does everything half-assed.*

- *I am going to lose my ever-loving shit over this. I cannot take this anymore.*

I trust you see the pattern that's developing here. I also trust that you have had a similar discussion, at some point or another, in your own mind. If not about a teen, then about your spouse, your boss, your best friend, your neighbor, or the guy driving in front of you on the freeway.

Now let's reappraise.

- *Maggie is a kid, so stuff like this isn't important to her. When she has her own place, she'll feel differently.*
- *Maggie is so busy with school and her social life; she must have dashed out after she vacuumed.*
- *I must make Maggie nuts with this kind of stuff; it must seem so silly.*
- *This might not bother me so much if I weren't so hormonal right now.*

Do you see where I'm going with this? It's all fantasy. Every bit. You don't know what's in Maggie's head. She doesn't know what's in yours. The fact that she didn't wind up the cord did, indeed, occur. All the rest of it—the whole death spiral of thought, judgment, feeling, and potential action—is a reaction to that stimulus based on imaginings. It is not fact. It's all your own.

By the way, before I left the store, I asked Maggie how the story had played out between her and her mom.

She said, "Oh, good. So good. We talked all about it and she told me how her hormones made her feel. And I talked about mine. Once we said it out loud, things between us were totally cool."

BAM.

Okay, so we're making it through the Mad Girl Math now. You can see how these equations are so interrelated, and how they could be so damn dangerous during PrimeTime. A little recap:

MY THOUGHTS ≠ REALITY

MY THOUGHTS = BULLSHIT

MY FEELINGS ≠ FACTS

MY FEELINGS = REACTIONS TO STIMULI

It's time to move on to the third equation, which—when answered correctly—is my favorite of them all.

CHAPTER 7

My Past = X

DNF

I used to be a quitter. To be more specific, I quit hard things. I've always managed to stick with the fun stuff (like vodka). But with more difficult stuff, I'd give up. I'd make it so far, circumstances would turn a little dicey, and I'd bow out.

Not only did I see myself as a quitter, my husband saw me as a quitter. He loved me. But we both knew I was a flake. Everyone else who loved me also knew I was a flake. The quitter part of me? She lived inside my head. She spoke to me. I often allowed her to call the shots and plan my future. I called her DNF, which is endurance-athlete-speak for "did not finish."

In 2012, when I was 45, I signed up for an Ironman 70.3 triathlon. I did it for a couple of reasons. First, I was just kind of done with all the reverence being paid to my Ironman husband. He was a little too big for his britches, and I needed a moment where I had the upper hand. Where I could say, "Oh, come on, Jan. It can't be that hard. If you can do it, I can do it!"

But the bigger reason was my vivid memory of watching Julie Moss on *The Wide World of Sports* when I was in the tenth grade. In one of the most spectacular displays of female badassery in history, then 23-year-old Julie was solidly in first place in the Ironman race in Kona, Hawaii when her legs gave out beneath her on the run, and she collapsed onto the course. Utterly exhausted and entirely spent, in the dark of night, she was just a few hundred yards from the finish line when she first fell. After more than 12 hours and 140 miles of racing, she fought her way to her feet... and collapsed again. As spectators and race officials stepped forward to help her, she shook them off, forced herself to stand, and hobbled forward.

She would fall three more times on her way to the finish. With the end of the race literally in sight, Julie was on the ground when her closest competitor ran past her and snagged the victory. In a spectacular show of will, Julie crawled on her hands and knees through a throng of screaming spectators, and threw herself over the line.

Even more amazing? Thirty-five years later, Julie Moss is *still* crushing it in Ironman races. And these days, when she returns to Kona for the World Championship races, she competes in the 55-59 age division, as an astonishingly powerful symbol of PrimeTime.

Can you see why I wanted a piece of Ironman?

I wanted to ache for something so badly that I'd crawl to get it. I wanted to have that feeling for my very own.

I did, however, face several challenges related to competing in a triathlon: I could not swim. I could not ride a bike. And I was an extremely slow runner. I also had a history of quitting when the going got tough, and was at least 20 pounds overweight. Still, I somehow assessed this as an entirely realistic goal. So Jan and I registered for the Ironman 70.3 race in Haines City, Florida. It would be a 1.2-mile swim, followed by a 56-mile bike ride and a 13.1-mile run.

In preparation for the event, I did 16 weeks of hard training made up of about 90 workouts. DNF was there with me, in my head, for every one. She mocked me and chided me from bell to bell. She's a bitch. She's the queen of criticism and reproach, the master of the head game, and the evil twin to my "let's do this shit" side. But I had to let her hang out with me—we had history.

About four weeks prior to the big Florida race, I participated in my first official event—The Rage Triathlon in Henderson, Nevada. Rage was an Olympic-distance race— exactly half the total mileage I would be covering in my Ironman event. Jan agreed to rage with me.

DNF rode with us in the car, checked in with me at the hotel, and started jabbering the moment I woke up on race day. She was with me when I walked into the transition area, where we "athletes" racked our bikes. I had never been "in transition." The experience was a total rush. I'm pretty sure the adrenaline surge intimidated DNF.

With my signature obsessiveness, I laid out my bike shoes and socks, running shoes and hat, sunscreen and race belt, and all the other little items I'd purchased at top price from designer triathlon labels. In the event there would be a trophy for neatness, I would definitely snag it.

Lake Meade sparkled before us—vast, blue, and cruel— and I was seriously edgy about the first leg of the race. I did not swim well—not fast, not straight, not with any kind of actual technique. I was also embarrassingly inexperienced with my wet suit; the two times I'd worn it prior had involved a physical fight between myself and the preposterously tight neoprene. Both bouts had ended with me cased in rubber, standing in a pile of sweat and tears. The experience was no more graceful on race day, and DNF was already making her case for the big quit as I wriggled, grunted, and stomped.

The water froze my feet as I stood in the shallows waiting for the gun to go off. I don't even remember the start. But I sure as shit remember my first rookie mistake. It happened about 750 meters in, when I swam straight past the buoy that marked the halfway point. The point where we were supposed to turn around.

I had trained in a swimming pool with lines painted on the bottom for guidance. I'd been warned by my coach that lake swimming was much different. So I used the "sighting" method I'd been taught, which involved looking up every third or fourth stroke, and catching sight of a marker along the course.

Experienced swimmers know how to remain afloat when they use this method. Stroke, stroke, sight. Stroke, stroke, sight. Not me. I stopped kicking and let my legs fall far beneath the water every time I looked up. Stroke, stroke, sight, sink. Stroke, stroke, sight, sink.

The other swimmers moved out ahead of me. It didn't seem the least bit odd that I was the last swimmer in the race by such a long shot. I just kept on keepin' on.

It wasn't until a helpful gentleman in a canoe approached me that I realized the literal error of my ways.

"Where you goin'?" he asked. *What a stupid, fucking question*, I thought.

"You tell me," I sputtered. "You're the one in the boat."

He pointed back to the missed buoy.

I wasn't sure how far off-course I swam—spatial abilities are not among my core competencies—but I guessed at least 50 or 100 yards. I turned around and swam a terribly slow, painfully embarrassing breaststroke to the finish. The whole time, DNF was whispering, "It hurts. This SUCKS. Triathlon is not for you. Just quit now." I couldn't shut her up, but I managed to ignore her and drag myself, breathless, onto the sand. Then another prissy girl fight with the wet suit, and a stumble back to the transition area.

I had worried about the bike *start* more than the bike *ride* from the first day of training. I'd locked my feet into pedals for the first time only 16 weeks earlier, and I'd never gotten used to the locks. I always felt like someone had tied me to the bike, and I was desperate to break free. I could never seem to get the hang of that first pedal stroke for momentum.

I was the last person left in the transition area.

Many moons ago, I memorized what I believe is the most powerful line in the *Desiderata* by Max Ehrmann. I pulled it out of my mental file cabinet, right then and there.

> If you compare yourself with others, you may become vain and bitter; for always there will be greater and lesser persons than yourself. Enjoy your achievements as well as your plans.

I told myself, *Last is okay. Last is still in the race. I don't even know these other people, for Christ's sake. I'll never see them again.*

I got on the bike and struggled to gain momentum as I pedaled up the hill toward the top of the transition area. *What kind of rocket scientist puts the transition area at the bottom of a fucking hill?!*

Then a race official shouted at me, "You can't mount your bike until you reach the green line. You have to get off the bike and remount."

So naturally, I hit my brakes. Fully forgetting that my feet were locked in the pedals. And I fell over. HARD. Right at the start line. I didn't even crash. I *fell over* at the green line, in front of a moderately large crowd.

A spectator yelled to me, "Get mad! Use it. Use it to your advantage!" I used that moment, instead, to get mad at him.

When exhaustion turns to humiliation, it's impossible to remember the *Desiderata*. I wasn't comparing myself to the other competitors in the race anymore. I was comparing myself to everyone else in the *world*. And I was the consummate moron.

DNF was chuckling now. I found her revolting.

I got up though. And I biked out. To the first massive hill. Not only was it dauntingly steep, but totally unexpected. An experienced triathlete would have ridden or driven the bike course before the race. But I'd skipped that. Everyone knows the desert is flat, right? For Christ's sake.

The first hill became a second hill, then a third and a fourth, and my emotions swung between defeated and terrified. I impelled myself up the hills with all the force I could muster, then held on with a death grip, braking all the way down. (If you're using this as a reference for your own future triathlon, most bicycles have *two* rings of multiple gears. And it's best to learn how to use every one of them before you ride hills.)

I biked for 45 minutes, afraid to drink or eat. The roads were open, cars were flying by, some were honking, and I was waiting for Ashton Kutcher to jump out at any moment to tell me I'd been Punk'd.

I pedaled and talked to myself. I said the Hail Mary in Latin and I solved math problems. I focused on anything I possibly could to avoid acknowledging DNF. But at Mile 11,

I made the mistake of speaking back to her for the first time that day. I engaged.

She was nearly singing now, a snotty little girl with a jump rope, telling me how she'd been right all along, and how I was a loser. She told me how good the beer on the other side of the finish line would taste... if only I'd *quit*. She told me how great air conditioning would feel... once I *quit*. She promised me that no one would ever know but me.

I argued with her. I told her I'd prepared sufficiently, I had a *right* to be there. I told her she was pure evil. But I was out-matched. DNF could have been a member of the Harvard debate team. She'd perfected her tone watching Joan Crawford in *Mommie Dearest*. She was fucking relentless.

So I stopped. I pulled off the road while headed up a steep incline. I got off the bike. I gulped water, and I cried. I bawled like a little girl, right there on a rocky desert highway in the middle of a triathlon called Rage. The tears rolled down for about a minute. Then I wiped my snotty nose with my $80 designer bicycle glove and climbed back on the bike.

I was feeling terribly sorry for myself and fully engaged in the war in my head when I locked my feet in and began to pedal uphill from a dead stop. And I fell over. For the second time that day.

As I lay there mortified, I let DNF take over. I went right ahead and allowed her to call the shots for the day. I quit.

Moments later, two race officials on a motorcycle drove up and asked if I was stopping. I found it so merciful that they didn't call it quitting. (There must be some kind of triathlon volunteer sensitivity training.) They ever-so-kindly radioed for a park ranger to pick me up.

During the 20-minute wait, my sweat dried, and in its place, I allowed shame to wash over me completely. The ride back to the transition area in the Nevada Parks and Recreation SUV was surreal. DNF was positively gloating.

Jan saw me climb out of the car. He saw me practically throw my bicycle into the rocks. He saw me stomp toward the transition area, fighting back sobs. And he did something I just didn't expect. He opened up his arms and pulled me into them.

He said what I hadn't considered. Not in that moment. Possibly not ever.

"Don't make this a bad thing. This was not your race. This was just part of your training plan."

As I stood there, hot and humiliated, defeated and broken, I realized he was right. That quitting today needn't mean giving up entirely. That DNF was *in* me, but she was *not* me. I just hadn't finished what I'd started. Yet.

We drove back to the hotel and did what real athletes do. We went to the bar. And together, Jan and I spent the afternoon with frosty mugs, reliving what I *had* done, rather than what I hadn't. The bike course had included 3,300 feet of vertical climbing, of which I'd completed nearly half, without ever properly shifting. I'd finished the swim in just over my anticipated time, despite the extra distance.

Jan had finished first in his age group that day. He took third overall. He didn't even tell me this until we'd finished our beers and the trophy ceremony had passed without him. He gave up his moment so he could teach me how to interpret mine.

The Rage Triathlon was nothing compared to the big show that was to come. I'd simply completed a *trial*. The whole purpose of a trial was to learn and make future course corrections.

Exactly 30 days later, I crossed the finish line at the Ironman 70.3 in Florida. I was blessed with a beautiful, hot, sunny day and a totally flat course. Lance Armstrong was in the race too. Jan earned a personal record. I came in 1,998th out of 2,000 racers. It took me every minute of the eight and a half hours the Ironman rule book allowed.

When I rounded the corner to the finish, I saw that Jan had amassed an entire crowd of strangers to cheer for me. They were chanting my name. He was yelling, "Go, baby, go!" He was laughing. And he was crying. It was fucking glorious.

DNF was there too. She pretended to be happy for me. But I knew we wouldn't be seeing much of each other after that. Too much water under the bridge.

I was a quitter, until the day that I wasn't. Until the day I learned that I'd been duped by the last of the Mad Girl Math equations:

MY PAST = MY FUTURE

It does not, my friend. It most certainly does not.

YOU ARE A BEST-SELLER

When you can solve this last math problem correctly, you'll be well on the way to whatever you want. But if you solve it the way most Mad Girls do (MY PAST = MY FUTURE), you'll talk yourself out of anything big that you've ever dreamt of.

Not only does your past NOT equal your future, it is not even a reliable *predictor* of your future. It doesn't even provide an adequate definition of who you are *today*. Because your past doesn't exist anymore. It is no longer real. Except in your thoughts. And in your feelings. (I think we've adequately covered what you can do with those.)

Your past is what they refer to in fiction as your "backstory." I encourage you to see it like a fiction writer would, because it will free you to write a future story with deliberation, determination, and imagination.

In fiction, the backstory is the story *before* the story. It's invented by the writer to give the future story depth. When you read a work of fiction, you don't always know the character's backstory, but the writer knows. Even though she'll never share it completely with the reader, the writer has most definitely *created* it.

A fiction writer creates a backstory for every character in her novel, to help her fill in the gaps. To support where the character is *going*. To help you, the reader, get behind the character. To make you sympathetic to the character. To convince you to believe in the character. The backstory isn't the story. It's where the story *begins*.

Now this part is critical, so listen up. A backstory has an *infinite* number of possible future stories. A relationship does exist between the backstory and the future story. But it is not a *cause and effect* relationship. Unless you demand that this be so, the way a Mad Girl would.

Let's say our fiction writer has a character in her novel whose backstory includes drug use, a little prison time, and maybe a bit of porn. Must the future story be about a snuff film that takes place in a meth trailer? Fuck no. It could be about a mother who loves her child so fiercely that she cleans herself up and puts herself through med school to support her child's dreams. In this case, the backstory would just make you like the character more because she got over herself and started taking brave action.

Or it could be about a woman and her dad who work to form the close relationship they never had and, through the process, the woman finds herself in rehab, where she meets the man of her dreams. (Here the backstory would make you like her better because she'd finally taken responsibility for herself, and had begun taking brave action.)

You are the writer of your future story.

Your past does not dictate the future. It gives your future depth. It provides context and an interesting framework. It teaches you lessons that you might want to *apply* to your future. But it is not your fucking future.

Your past is over. It's finished. It defines who you were in the moment *before* this one.

So let's review that math.

$$MY\ PAST \neq MY\ FUTURE$$
$$MY\ PAST = HISTORY$$

HOW THE FUTURE IS FORMED

Do you know what *does* dictate your future? Your actions.

I feel compelled to take a moment here to buck a current trend that focuses on embracing failure. I read a lot of books that highly recommend failing. Failing is fashionable right now. They say, "Fail forward. Fail fast. You must fail in order to succeed."

That's terrible advice. Fuck failure. It feels yucky. It sucks you dry. It comes with a bunch of self-recrimination and sometimes blame, and it's generally a horrible experience. Don't embrace failure!

Instead, become wholly comfortable with concept of *trials*. More specifically, trials and course corrections.

Any big goal, project, or feat that you want to complete can—and must—be broken into a series of smaller trials. It doesn't matter if you want to become the best belly dancer in the tri-city area, find the man of your dreams, or make the perfect six-course Italian meal. Every successful endeavor is broken down this same way.

First, you conduct a small trial. Then you take what you learned (this is where the past is useful), and you correct your course for the next trial. It's a path of discovery. It's a learn-as-you-go kind of process. It's a proven and time-tested system for achieving whatever's in your heart. And it's fun!

Trial. Course correction. Trial. Course correction. And so on.

If you learn to view your actions as trials, you embrace a beginner's mind. And a beginner's mind is curious. It's playful. It's light-hearted. It yearns to explore.

Have you ever seen a toddler take a few steps, fall down, and think to herself, *Fuck it. I'm done. I failed. Walking is not for me. I'll just crawl forever?* No. You have not. Because toddlers have beginners' minds. They are open, they are eager, and they are entirely devoid of all that nasty and sickening judgment.

So before you move on from this chapter, you've got a bit of work to do. Because it's the key to making the rest of this book your bitch. Don't skip it. Don't gloss over it. If you do, someday you'll be giving your dream over to the snotty little girl with the jump rope inside your own head. And you are so much better than that.

1. Write the future story of your own PrimeTime. You don't need to write 5,000 words. No one will read it but you. Just write it. And if you don't want to write it, download a free recorder app on your phone and speak it into that. Say what it looks like, feels like, tastes like, sounds like, and smells like when Prime-Time is in full swing and you have what you want.

2. Use your backstory for depth. Develop a character for that future story who you can support and talk up. One you can sympathize with. One who makes you cry because she's so authentic and amazing. One who makes you stand up and cheer because she's so brave. Your future story begins right in this moment. So you can make that character behave any way you choose.

3. Make a list of 21 small trials—specific, detailed actions—that you will complete to move yourself toward what you desire. One trial per day, for 21 days. And agree to conduct your first trial tomorrow. (After 21 days, you'll be on a roll, my friend.)

4. Decide, in this moment, that you are now the woman who will complete these trials. You are the woman shaped by your backstory, and committed to your future story. You are the woman who is curious, open, eager, searching, and willing to course correct.

5. Read your story (or listen to the recording you made), and say this out loud, "It will be so."

Then sit for a minute and soak up what I say next, because once you come to know it—deep in your heart and your bones—you will never be the same.

The only way you will fail at reaching your goal is if you refuse to take action or quit before your trials are complete.

There is simply no other way to fail.

As you complete your trials, you will be attacked by a litany of shitty thoughts.

Remember this:

MY THOUGHTS ≠ REALITY

MY THOUGHTS = BULLSHIT

As you complete your trials, you will find yourself buried beneath a landslide of feelings.

Remember this:

MY FEELINGS ≠ FACTS

MY FEELINGS = REACTION TO STIMULI

As you complete your trials, you will tell yourself that you've never done anything like this before, and that you are not the kind of person who can do this.

Remember this:

MY PAST ≠ MY FUTURE

MY PAST = HISTORY

You are no longer a Mad Girl. You are a PrimeTime star. Now we've gotta do something about your lying.

CHAPTER 8

A Brand Built on Lies

RED WINE BY THE BAG

At this point, you should have a pretty solid grasp on the fact that your thoughts, your feelings, and your beliefs about the past are limiting you. But what I haven't touched on yet is something so much bigger that's holding you back. It's a distinct set of lies that modern society has taught you to believe about middle age. I call them the Six Lies that Bind.

These lies are every bit as popular as they are horrible. Almost every PrimeTime woman I know believes them, in some form or another. What's worse, we *tell* them. We repeat them. To ourselves and to others.

I first stumbled upon the Six Lies that Bind on the night I spilled an entire glass of Pinot Noir into my purse. The dark, sticky mess that ensued led me to an eventual clean slate. But I need to back up just a bit, to bring you into the loop.

At the time I started searching for my big PrimeTime purpose, I was running my own branding agency. Thirteen years earlier (after I'd screwed the intern in a hot summer fling, fled to the desert with my career in ashes, then married the intern and had his son), I'd started my own business. And I'd developed successful brand strategies for some pretty big corporations.

By PrimeTime, I had a national automotive client that provided a substantial chunk of my agency's income. For about five years, that account had been reliable and steady. Until the day I got the call. It came just weeks after I'd received that fated call from Stuart Grauer on Mastery Learning Day. Due to a major shift in my client's retail strategy, they no longer needed my agency's services. In a split second, I watched hundreds of thousands of dollars walk right out the door.

I knew I had a choice to make. The same one that I'd faced scores of times before in the brutal cycle of the agency business. I could put on my navy-blue suit, start knocking on boardroom doors, replace the account, and carry on. Or not.

But this time, it felt different. I was 47 years old. No part of me wanted to create a PowerPoint presentation, generate a portfolio, hock my wares, or sell my soul. No part of me wanted to help another big corporation stuff more dollar bills into its pockets.

After several tearful talks with Jan and the creative team that was working on the account, I turned my back on corporate America for the last time. I shut down the agency. And in its place, over the course of about 60 days, I built a blog site.

I used my new blog to teach budding entrepreneurs about branding. Every morning I woke up and wrote about what I knew, and about what I thought small business owners should know. At first, no one read my shit but Jan, my mom, and three of my girlfriends. But I pressed on, shouting into what was essentially a deep, dark, empty hole.

I also locked myself in the bathroom for several weeks (the only place in the house where I was guaranteed silence and some decent acoustics) and created a 25-lesson online course to teach entrepreneurs in 6 weeks what I'd learned about branding over a 25-year career.

The course and the blog were well received. And little by little, my audience grew.

Although I hadn't intentionally set out to do so, I attracted women almost exclusively. What I hadn't realized, until the night that glass of Pinot dumped into my purse, was that my followers weren't just exclusively *women*. They were mostly middle-aged women. Women like me.

The night of the big spill, Jan and I had met some friends for happy hour at a local restaurant called Craftsman. It's one of those dark, industrial-looking places with giant wine racks and hard wooden stools that seem super hip, but that no one with an ass the size of mine wants to sit on. The kind of place with cement floors and high ceilings, where everyone practically screams to be heard.

As soon as my first glass of Pinot took hold, the laughs began, I got loud, and I started waving my hands around to punctuate the story I was telling. So when the waitress set my second glass on the table, it took me all of two seconds to knock it over.

I watched in horror as nine ounces of grapey goodness spilled out of the glass and straight into my beautiful new black leather clutch purse, which sat open on the stool next to me. I stopped talking, and the thoughts started rolling.

Can I still carry the purse? It's black. It will dry. You can't really tell.

If I carry it, will the moms at school know?

Will I smell like Pinot Noir?

Will they even care?

Doesn't every mom drink Pinot Noir?

Do I even want to hang out with moms who don't drink Pinot Noir?

Had any of the hot younger women in the joint seen me do this?

Were they laughing at me?

Did I look ridiculous and feeble?

When had I become such a desperate, self-conscious, "older" woman?

When would the waitress be back to pour me another glass of Pinot Noir?

And would she give it to me for free... out of pity?

As it turns out, the waitress did replace that second glass of Pinot Noir at no charge. And I had her bring me a third, which is almost never a good idea. But on this night, that third glass somehow cracked me open. In the Uber on the way home, I started to mentally unpack and examine all those questions I'd asked myself in the moment of the big spill, and about a thousand others. I started to wonder why I was so jacked up about what people thought of me. About what I had become at this age.

In through that crack crept the truth. I hadn't just shut down my agency because of a desire to start something new and exciting. I'd also done it because I was afraid. I was afraid that if I *had* gone knocking on those boardroom doors at the age of 47, I would have been too old to land those accounts. That if my agency had been pitted against one led by a younger woman, I would have lost out. Or that if I'd had to hire a younger woman to run my shop, I would have lost face. I was afraid that in a world of tweets, likes, clicks, shares, Facebook live feeds, and Snapchats, I was lagging, and I could never catch up.

I stumbled through the front door of my house that night and made a totally reckless but seriously game-changing move. I wrote a blog post and an email to my entire list of 35,000 women. Right there in the kitchen, with my buzz on, my heart open, and my handbag reeking of the Russian River Valley.

I didn't give branding advice, which is what my readers had all signed on for. I just talked. As though I were talking to my closest friends. I confessed about spilling the wine into my purse. I admitted how I'd come to feel diminished, self-conscious, and disconnected. I made a list of all the things that I needed to finally let go, if I were to be truly happy in middle age. I poured my heart out just as the wine had poured out of that glass.

At the end of the email, I asked those women a single question: **What do you need to let go?**

Then I hit Send and went to bed.

THE MORNING AFTER

I'd left my laptop on the counter next to the espresso machine. In the morning, I shuffled to the kitchen and pushed the button for two large espressos. As the sound of the bean grinder drowned out the pounding in my head, I looked over at the screen. And I nearly peed my pants.

As I'd headed off to bed the night before, the women in the UK and France had just been waking up. The women in Australia had been eating dinner. They had opened the email when it landed in their inboxes. And they had responded. In droves.

I scrolled through a list of emails that just kept going. Emails from Kathy, Brenda, Laurie, Valerie, Anaya, Lois, Chantel, Olivia, Pari, Maxine, LaToya, Maria... The emails were still sliding into my inbox in that very moment, as the women on the East Coast responded. And messages continued to pour in all throughout the morning, as the women on the West Coast woke up and joined the party. More than 200 women responded that day. Every one of them had something that they needed to let go in middle age.

As the caffeine began to kick in, the truth began to sink in. My purpose wasn't to talk to these incredible women about the brands they were building for their businesses. Instead, they needed to share the experiences that had diminished them in middle age. The fears that were holding them back from what they truly wanted. The ludicrous assumptions and judgments that society was holding over them.

Some were laughing. Some were angry. Some felt hopeless. They were all total strangers. Yet they told me their secrets. They told me heart-wrenching stories of abuse and betrayal. Stories about insults they'd experienced at work or hurt feelings they couldn't seem to set aside. They spoke of their aging bodies and how they felt overlooked, ignored, unworthy, or unloved. Though their stories were different, they all shared a single experience: They had been *branded* as middle-aged women.

THE LIES OF THE "MIDDLE-AGED WOMAN" LABEL

Branding is about messaging. It's about a company articulating a message so perfectly that potential customers not only relate to it, they internalize it. They own it. They buy the product, and they *become* the brand. In a frighteningly real way, we *are* our smart phones, our jeans, our cars, our breakfast cereal, the music we listen to, and the vodka that we drink.

A brand is nothing more than what people think of or feel when they hear a name or see a label. What do you think of when you hear Mercedes? Or Jimmy Choo? Or Tiffany? Or

Apple? Your thoughts, your beliefs, your perceptions—they *define* those brands. And when you buy them, you allow them to define *you*. Labels are immensely powerful.

Let me ask you another question. What do you think of when you hear the label "middle-aged woman"?

If you're anything like the women I talked to while researching this book, your feelings about the "middle-aged woman" label are lukewarm at best and shitty at worst. I haven't met one woman who says, "God, I can't wait to be middle-aged. That shit is sexy. I'm gonna wear it to the party on Saturday night."

Corporations generally rebrand—and reach out to companies like mine for help—when they're in one of two situations. 1) They've experienced some kind of trouble, scandal, or problem, and buyers' opinions of the brand have become negative. Oftentimes it's because a secret has been revealed or because they've been "found out." Or 2) The marketplace has progressed or shifted, and the brand is outdated and struggling to keep up.

Both situations apply to the "middle-aged woman" label. This is a brand that—in today's world—exists entirely based on lies. Complete and utter lies. Additionally, the world has massively shifted where middle age is concerned. Middle-aged women are more powerful and viable than they've been at any time in history. Our brand is entirely outdated.

When these kinds of disconnections are exposed for a retail brand, customers just stop believing the bullshit. They stop buying the label. And the brand dies out. But what's remarkable about "middle-aged woman" is that it's still hanging on, in spite of its utter inaccuracy. In spite of the lies.

"Lie" is a super-charged word, I know. And many in the marketing industry would use a softer term. But I chose "lie" for a specific reason. Lies are special. They're purposeful.

Google the word *lie*, and you'll find two definitions in the pop-up dictionary:

1. An intentionally false statement
2. A situation involving deception or founded on a mistaken impression

Pick whichever definition makes you feel least comfortable. This is a brand built on lies. Companies that sell products to middle-aged women repeat the lies. They use the lies to access our insecurities and touch on our pain. They use the lies to incite fear and induce need. They use the lies to connect with us on a visceral level.

How was the "middle-aged woman" brand built? It started when the average life span was 49, 55, or 60. At a time when women went through menopause, then they *died*. Guess what, my beautiful friend? The world has shifted. We're not dying so young anymore. We're living another 30 years after menopause. But this old brand message, it lives on in glorious fashion.

Who continues to promote the outdated version of the "middle-aged woman"? A fuck-ton of people, that's who. The anti-aging industry promotes it so we'll buy wrinkle creams, suck out our cellulite, and shoot shit into our faces. The media promotes it so they can sell us magazines with tips and tutorials on how to look younger, feel younger, live younger...even have sex like we're younger. Silicon Valley promotes it when they equate innovation with youth, or when they treat people like assets that depreciate with age. The corporate world promotes it when they favor younger employees over those with wisdom and experience. Middle-aged men promote it, as they trade in PrimeTime women for younger models to address their own middle-age struggles.

A whole lot of hands promote the outdated "middle-aged woman" brand. Each one would have you believe that middle age is a dreadful phase in life and that you should do whatever you can to pretend it's not happening—avoid it, stall it, apologize for it, lie about it, and cover it up. A whole lot of money and energy have been thrown out to bolster this message.

The entire machine capitalizes on these Six Lies that Bind:

1. The Lie of Noble Selflessness
2. The Lie of Irrelevance
3. The Lie of Extenuating Circumstances
4. The Lie of Impropriety
5. The Lie of the Empty Hourglass
6. The Lie of Diminished Capacity

I will break down each one of these lies. I'll also show you how we become slaves to them and how the world profits from them. But before I do, I need you to see something else. Another huge culprit in the promotion of this nonsense. Ourselves.

FEATURES AND BENEFITS

Ultimately, brands are created and promoted because they lead to sales. Every transaction has two parties: the buyer and the seller. In the case of the Six Lies that Bind, once we buy the lies, we OWN the lies. We become the liars ourselves. We reinforce the message. We lie to ourselves, to each other, and to the world.

We own these lies for two reasons. First, they are prolific. They're everywhere. They are woven into our culture. Into the images we see, the stories we hear, the movies we watch, the books we read. We are bombarded with them, and they somehow begin to make sense. They are well crafted and easy to believe.

The second reason may be even more powerful than the first. Every time we tell ourselves one of these lies, we *get* something. We don't get the awesome thing we want for ourselves in PrimeTime. And we don't find happiness. But we walk away with *something*.

We may latch on to a feeling of significance. We feel that we are noble, principled, magnanimous, or moral when we live out these lies. We kick ourselves right to the curb so we can feel like martyrs or "good girls."

We may finagle permission to play the victim card. We can use it in negotiations later, to work our way into other things we want.

We may be able to remain certain about something. We play along and do what we're told, so we know exactly how a story will unfold. Certainty can be a comforting feeling. It's risk-free.

We may obtain the illusion of control. When we tell ourselves these lies, we set our own needs aside, which gives us plenty of time and energy to poke around in someone else's business.

Or, most dangerously, the lies give us permission to surrender to *resistance*.

My favorite inspirational writer is Steven Pressfield. Whenever I'm stuck, I pull out his wildly acclaimed *The War of Art*, and it unsticks me. Pressfield has a theory about what he calls "resistance." In his book *Do the Work*, he says:

> Remember, our enemy is not lack of preparation; it's not the difficulty of the project or the state of the marketplace or the emptiness of our bank account.
>
> The enemy is resistance.
>
> The enemy is our chattering brain, which, if we give it so much as a nanosecond, will start producing excuses, alibis, transparent self-justifications, and a million reasons why we can't/shouldn't/won't do what we know we need to do.

The Six Lies that Bind are resistance for PrimeTime women. When your chattering brain tells you why you can't do what you want or have what you want, the chatter will show up in the form of these six horrible lies. Because the lies are so familiar, they will occur to you as though they are your *own* thoughts. And if you are unprepared, you will entertain them.

Then your feelings will show up. The spin cycle will begin. And you will press the pause button on your fun, freaky, PrimeTime future without a second of consideration. Let me show you how we come to own a well-engineered lie and use it as resistance.

WHAT WILL IT TAKE TO GET YOU TO BUY TODAY?

Long before I learned about branding, I was exposed to sales. My dad was an old-school car dealer. The kind who would say, "Whaddya think, we plug these lights into the moon?" or "Whaddya mean you have to ask your *wife* if you can buy a car?"

He carried a wad of cash in his pocket with a rubber band around it. He wore adjustable-waistband Sansabelt slacks and perfectly coordinated polyester-blend golf shirts that stretched across his generous belly. He golfed 18 holes most afternoons, and spent his evenings in dark lounges with high-back red leather booths and enormous porterhouse steaks. After 8:00 p.m., he invariably had his short, square fingers wrapped around a glass of something clear, amber, and on the rocks.

In the 1970s, his dealership broke Datsun's sales record for the highest number of new vehicles sold in a single month.

By the time he died in 2008, Datsun had become Nissan, but the record still stood. He was the consummate influencer.

From my dad, I inherited the gift of gab, my sarcastic wit, and Popeye's arms and legs. I also inherited his innate understanding of what makes people tick, which is a ninja weapon for succeeding in sales.

When, as a college freshman, I decided to major in creative writing, he suggested I come on down to the dealership and learn sales, "just in case I wasn't Hemingway." There he taught me two lessons that are especially pertinent when it comes to the next six chapters of this book. Understanding these two concepts will help you understand why you've come to own the lies.

First, people don't buy things. Rather, they buy the way those things will make them *feel*. Second, contrary to what you may believe, most people don't make major purchase decisions after considerable research and forethought. Instead, they buy things on whims, driven by intense emotional triggers.

When we buy products that capitalize on the "middle-aged woman" label, we're not buying creams or plastic surgery or uglier, more appropriate shoes. What we're buying are the lies. We also buy the lies when we believe what past generations, the media, or our own fears tell us about middle age. And when we settle for less than we want in PrimeTime.

Over the past two years of working with PrimeTime women, I've come to realize we buy the Six Lies that Bind the same way we buy cars. The engineering of these lies is so complex and sophisticated that it would put BMW to shame. And the reasons we buy them (the cars and the lies) have everything to do with the way we need to feel in any given moment.

Allow me to demonstrate how a great lie is engineered, sold, and then driven around by us. So you can see the intricacy of the machines at work and understand how they both seduce us and provide a service. In the car business, we call this "walk-around training." Watch me walk around the lies and demonstrate exactly what they offer you.

THE ENGINE

A well-engineered lie is built to last. You can drive it for a lifetime, and sometimes you will. It holds up mile after mile. But it's not just enduring, it's also reliable. You can count on a good lie to perform every single time. That's important, because a well-engineered lie has a purpose: It takes you where you want to go. It carries you from Point A to Point B. You just give it a little fuel, and it runs like a dream.

THE MODEL

A well-engineered lie comes in a variety of models to accommodate your lifestyle. You can find one with room for whomever you'd like to take along. Girls' road trip? No problem. The kids and the hubby? Absolutely. Your boss and coworkers? Check. You can even take the soccer team. Sometimes, you just want to ride in it all by yourself.

THE INTERIOR

But a well-engineered lie isn't just practical. It's got a fit and finish that's rich with intricate details. And in PrimeTime, we are extremely choosy about those details. Because while they accommodate both our needs and our idiosyncrasies, they also say a little bit about who we are as individuals.

THE CHASSIS DESIGN

A well-engineered lie is eye candy. It has style. Curves, strong lines, rich colors. We are not afraid to show it to the world. We can choose an exterior trim package that suits us and reflects our panache and sensibility.

THE TEST-DRIVE DEMONSTRATION

Allow me to demonstrate. Let's take the lie "I'm fine" for a little test drive. Although this is *not* one of the Six Lies that Bind, I know that you've been around the block in it a time or two, and that you bought it and took it home. I *saw* you at the dealership.

When you say, "I'm fine," you are usually not fine. You don't believe that you are fine. You feel, though, that's it's best to say you're fine. You do this either because you feel that you *should* be fine—based on what you've learned from the world—or because "I'm fine" brings you something. It might not deliver what you want, but it provides you with *something*.

"I'm fine" is a well-engineered lie. "I'm fine" makes Elon Musk look like a fucking amateur. Without a doubt, it's built to last. Most of us have relied on "I'm fine" since we were old enough to drive.

And by God, "I'm fine" will move you from A to B like nobody's business. Whether you want to drive directly to the end of a conversation you're not enjoying, to the place where you can fume and feel sorry for yourself, or to the place where your husband knows that you are seriously pissed off, you can count on "I'm fine" to deliver you there. Every. Single. Time.

You might choose a more elaborate fit and finish, like "Don't worry about me, I'm fine" or a more practical upholstery that's easier for cleanup, like "Sure. It's fine." Or you could go with the black leather and tinted windows: "Seriously, Matthew. I'm *fine*."

"I'm fine" has room for everyone. You can take your kids, your husband, your boss, your neighbor, and even your mother-in-law along for the ride. Some women prefer more headroom, as offered in the "It's aaaall good" model or the sportier "That's cool" edition or even the crossover "No problem." I even know some women who drive the tough-as-nails, four-wheel-drive version with heavy-duty shocks: "Whatever."

Are you pickin' up what I'm puttin' down here? It doesn't matter what kind of metal and glass you wrap around it; it's all the same lie. Not a woman in the history of the world has ever said "I'm fine" because she was *actually* fine. This is a lie.

And it's a lie (rather than a story or a misrepresentation or a mindset) because it's *intentional*.

We tell the "I'm fine" lie with *purpose*. One of the biggest reasons we say, "I'm fine" is so we can avoid action. So we can find a way around the work that will propel us to "I'm amazing. I'm overjoyed. I'm fulfilled. And I'm rocking PrimeTime like a girl band on a world tour."

This is exactly the way the Six Lies that Bind work. We choose the model that works best for us, and we own it, based on how we feel in the present moment, or how we *want* to feel. We drive around in it, and draw out what we need from it. It's a crying, fucking shame.

Understanding that MY THOUGHTS ≠ REALITY and MY FEELINGS ≠ FACTS is critical in making your way past these lies. But you'll need more than that when you bump up against them. You will need to understand the truth.

CLEANING UP THE SPILL

After the Pinot Noir spill, I spent the whole day and most of the night answering every one of those 200 emails. I vowed that day to take on the biggest branding project of my career: rebranding "middle-aged woman."

But I need your help. I can't do it without you. It is up to US to expose the lies of the "middle-aged woman" label. It is up to us to show ourselves, each other, and the world that we will not be cast aside or held back.

Over the next six chapters, it will be my pleasure to introduce you to some seriously badass PrimeTime women. They will show you the truth about the Six Lies that Bind.

CHAPTER 9

The Lie of Noble Selflessness

THE SPIN CYCLE

My mom and dad were divorced and remarried—to each other—four times. My mom was pregnant at the senior prom, and by the time graduation day rolled around in June of 1956, Delino and Nancy had already tied the knot for the first time. Their fourth divorce was final in 1968. For all four divorces, they saw the same judge, who finally told my mom that if she was foolish enough to marry my father one more time, that she would not be granted a legal reprieve in his court room. I was 2 (and my brothers were 9, 11, and 12) when my dad skipped off to southern California to do his own thing, leaving Nancy to raise the four of us. I have no memories of him ever living in our house.

We saw my dad during summers and Christmas vacations, when we flew to San Diego. Nancy never got her own vacations, though, not the way "regular" divorced moms do. Because when I was 5, she met and married a man with three sons of his own. They were 2, 4, and 8. And during holidays, the lucky new couple swapped my mom's kids for his.

My mom put herself tenth. She came behind all seven kids, my stepdad, and even the whims of her ex who lived across the country. She would work all day as a secretary at the local public school, then come home and make amazing dinners from scratch. On a typical Tuesday night, we'd have hand-battered fried chicken, green beans, mashed potatoes, and corn with butter. We were allowed to bring anyone we wanted to dinner, so there would frequently be 10 or 12 kids around our dining room table.

I have a vivid memory of standing in the kitchen with my mom when I was about 8, watching her slave away to feed us. I told her flat out, "I will never cook like this. When I have kids, I'm going to hire a chef." (I knew by the second grade that utter selflessness was not my bag.)

I remember my childhood in two distinct periods. During period one (the mid- to late-70s) my three older brothers were in high school. The nation had moved on from the Summer of Love, but had left behind its remnants: Quaaludes, bennies, and blotter acid. It seemed as though the entire student body at Dublin High School generously partook of all those and more, and not only at parties. These kids were lighting up during math class. My brothers rode my mom so hard that I'm surprised she made it across the canyon. Someone was always being kicked out of school, threatened with juvenile detention, dropped off by the cops, or falling through the front door.

Nancy was certainly *not* one of those parents who looked the other way or buried her head in the sand. As best she could, she ran a tight fucking ship. Because I was only 6 or 7, I was frequently with her when she yanked my brothers (who were dressed in wide-collared polyester shirts, bell-bottoms, and four-inch platform shoes) out of unsupervised house parties.

She would jab her finger in their faces, the veins in her neck standing at attention, as she told them what she would not tolerate. She would nod in exhausted understanding as the principal warned of punishments for future shenanigans. I can remember once, in vivid color, sitting on the dotted vinyl back seat of our yellow VW Fastback as she drove like a madwoman right through a cornfield, chasing after one of my brothers, who was on foot.

The second period of my childhood began when I was a teen, after my older brothers had moved out and my step-brothers had moved in. *The Brady Bunch* was cancelled in 1974, but our family continued producing new episodes until 1989. And they were surely not appropriate for the After-School daypart. Although the wild parties had been replaced by family counseling sessions, they were equally as raucous.

Through both phases of my childhood, Nancy parented non-stop. She never missed a football game, spelling bee, garage band performance, parent-teacher conference, awards banquet, or crisis. She focused on nothing else in her life.

One thing I do *not* remember in our house—ever—was being tasked with regular chores. We had enough kids to manage a small farm. But my mom did all the work. If you asked Nancy, now or then, she'd tell you that's what she wanted. She chose to raise kids. And the day she had signed up for us, she had turned in her "me" card. Helen (her mother) had never parented my mom. She'd never shown her the love or understanding she deserved. And Nancy made up for it, a thousand times over, by loving us selflessly.

I went to Catholic school, so I had friends with 10, 12, and even 15 kids in their families. I know their moms had lives. They were in bridge clubs and played tennis. They bought themselves nice preppy clothes from Madison's department store at the toney Lane Avenue Shopping Center. But my mom never did. There was no room in our house for her needs, her yearnings, her health, or her sanity.

surely much of this was because of our situation with money. In short, we had none. We definitely could not rely on my dad's contributions, the size and frequency of which were determined by the number of cars he sold and how the bets went with his bookie on Sundays.

But dollars aside, Nancy's approach to child-rearing was essentially a matter of belief. We were entitled. Not only to her money, but to her love, her time, her attention, all of her emotions, and every bit of her energy.

That is, until she had a moment of PrimeTime brilliance one day in the laundry room, where she spent an inordinate amount of her time. On a weekday morning, nearly 25 years after she'd begun raising children, she saw a glimmer of truth that contradicted the first of the Six Lies that Bind, which I call the Lie of Noble Selflessness.

I was a high school sophomore, and we had just moved into a brand-new three-story townhome. Among other modern creature comforts that delighted us kids, our new place on Grandwoods Circle had a laundry chute. The benefits were beyond fantastic.

We could access the chute from the hallway on the third floor. And we did so with reckless abandon. Every morning before school, we scooped up all the clothes that were strewn across our beds and bedroom floors (regardless of whether they were dirty) and stuffed them into the chute. They would slide down past the second floor into the basement, where they would land in a pile on the floor.

On the morning that Nancy saw the light, none of us had any clean clothes. We'd begun barking at her the moment we woke up. She'd dragged herself down to the laundry room, as she often did, to throw a load into the washer before work. That's when we heard her screams from the basement.

We raced downstairs to find her shoving a broom handle up through the square hole in the ceiling. Dirty clothes covered every visible inch of the laundry room floor, in a layer that formed the base of a monstrous pile. It rose to a peak at the ceiling, where it disappeared into the hole. The chute itself was also packed tightly, all the way to the third floor. Nancy stood, screaming bloody murder, in 30 vertical feet of dirty laundry.

As we headed off to school about an hour later, she sat with her head in her hands at the kitchen table, sobbing. She had called in sick to do the laundry. We suspected she was cracking up. But we had grossly underestimated her.

Legend has it that as she worked her way through the sea of clothes and towels, Nancy vowed to *never* be in this situation again. She cursed her life and she cursed her kids, and she uncovered something that had been hidden deep inside her.

She also uncovered the roll of butcher paper and tempera poster paints that my cheerleading squad used to make the signs our varsity football players smashed through at games. She'd managed a trip to Kmart for some additional supplies as well.

When we walked into the house around four o'clock that afternoon, an eight-foot banner stretched across the living room wall. It read, "Attention Residents: The Laundry Lady Has Resigned." Nancy sat on the couch, smiling serenely. Ten milligrams of Valium could not have produced a more trouble-free expression.

In front of her were four lawn-and-garden-sized trash cans and four laundry baskets with our names painted on them—one of each, for each of us. In the bottom of each laundry basket was an official typewritten memo providing us with a complete breakdown of the new self-reliance program to be implemented immediately. It also listed a choice of times we could report to the basement for our individual laundry lessons.

That was the last time Nancy ever did our laundry. We spent the next few years yanking one another's wet clothes from the dryer and tossing them onto the floor. Many a laundry room fight ensued, and some even became physical. But Nancy remained cool and calm in the I-don't-give-a-fuck space she'd so artfully created for herself. She did not engage, and we did not ask her to. She had made her position perfectly, painfully clear.

On that day, Nancy stopped telling herself the Lie of Noble Selflessness. She stopped telling herself, "I need to sacrifice my own happiness, so they can have theirs." She stopped telling herself that we always came first. That she would be less of a mom if we were more accountable for ourselves. That she would be giving up on us if she gave something to herself. On that day, the truth set Nancy free.

FOLLOW THE RED BOUNCING BALL

You might not have seven kids. You also might not give yourself away to the extent that Nancy did. But I'd be willing to bet that you tell yourself the Lie of Noble Selflessness. You don't even need to be a mom to tell it. You can put your boss first, your spouse first, your friends first, your own parents first, or even your cat first.

The Lie of Noble Selflessness comes in many different models.

My time will come.

These moments won't last forever. I need to give them to the kids.

My parents will be gone before I know it. I need to dedicate myself to them now.

If I want to be taken seriously, I need to put my career first.

Work is more important than sleep.

I took on that role when I signed up for this relationship.

My husband works so hard, I need to take care of him before me.

It's wrong to put myself first.

I don't deserve that.

Being a good mom (wife, leader, daughter, employee) is about real sacrifice.

If I focus on my own hopes and dreams, someone else will miss out.

I don't care what model you're driving, it's a lie.

I present the Lie of Noble Selflessness as the first lie, because every other lie hinges on it. If you continue to believe, in any way, that it's wrong for you to put yourself first, you will never have a chance. You will undoubtedly come to feel one of two nasty ways throughout PrimeTime. You'll either feel guilty (if you pursue what you want) or unfulfilled (if you don't). You may even feel angry or resentful.

This is your PrimeTime, my friend. Trust me when I tell you that you *can* have what you want. Without guilt, shame, or the need to explain.

The Lie of Noble Selflessness has a powerful sway over PrimeTime women, more than other people, because we were taught to believe it when we were children and we've been living it for decades. But we have reached a time in our lives when we can finally see space for an alternative possibility. We can almost taste what it feels like to fulfill our own desires and languish in what we want. We are so damn close!

But the lie was drilled into us. We were taught that being selfish is bad. Period. It is always noble to think of other people first. Putting your happiness behind someone else's is a virtue, right?

Bullshit.

Take a moment right now to close your eyes and think about when the Lie of Noble Selflessness leads you straight into sacrifice. Think about the either/or dilemmas in your life that are—in reality—nothing of the sort. Think of the moments when you say, "It's my happiness or theirs" even though it's not true. Think of the moments when you do things for others that they could—and should—do for themselves.

Imagine something as inconceivable as say, skipping your kids' soccer game because you have plans. How would you feel? Do you believe you must choose between being a "good mom" (or wife, boss, employee, daughter, sister, friend) and being *satisfied*?

I love to use Harry Browne's analogy when I talk about this lie, because it so clearly demonstrates why selflessness is not a logical concept. In Browne's book *How I Found Freedom in an Unfree World*, he says to consider happiness as a red rubber ball that you're holding in your hands. Because you were programmed to believe that it's bad to be selfish, you toss the ball of happiness to your friend. But she's also been taught to be selfless, so she tosses the happiness to someone else. And that person tosses the happiness to her children. Because they're taught to be selfless, they feel like they should pass on the happiness as well. And you can see where this goes.

The only reason to be selfless is so that someone can receive. There must be a taker. There must be a recipient of the selfless act. And if the whole world believes that selfishness is wrong, there will never be a taker. According to Browne, you fall into the "unselfishness trap" any time you neglect your own wants to avoid being labeled as selfish.

YOUR PERMISSION SLIP

For each of the Six Lies that Bind, I will uncover the truth. Remember how we reframed situations in the FEELINGS ≠ FACTS lesson? Remember cognitive reappraisal? If you believed the lie, you can just as easily believe the truth. The Lie of Noble Selflessness is a powerful one. But the truth is much more so. It comes in four parts. And it should give you total permission to do whatever makes you feel good. Even if someone else feels bad about it.

1. **You owe it to the universe to be happy.** You were given the gift of this life on Earth. If you give it away to someone else, you neither do it justice nor show gratitude for it. In fact, you thumb your nose at it.

   Imagine you bought me a gorgeous new cashmere sweater for my birthday. You spent time choosing the perfect sweater for me. You saw this sweater as an opportunity for me to look absolutely smashing. You wanted me to have it.

   Now imagine that the moment you gave it to me, I handed it over to my daughter, right in front of you, and said, "Here, honey, you can have this." Wouldn't you be seriously pissed?

   That's the way the universe feels when you give away your own happiness. The universe does not abide by this kind of senselessly selfless behavior.

   It is your job, your number one role on this Earth, to make the most of the life you have been given. A big part of that may be contribution to others. I am seriously down with that. What I am not down with is selflessness.

2. **You can't give something away that you don't have.** It is awfully hard to be fully present for anyone

else when you haven't shown up for yourself. If your cup is empty, you can't pour anything out of it. When you take care of yourself first, you have more energy, more imagination, more joy, and more attention to give.

On the extreme side of the Lie of Noble Selflessness lies codependency. Essentially, codependent people place the needs, health, and welfare of others before their own. They lose contact with their own needs, desires, and sense of self. In no way is this healthy or noble, but we learn it from generations of women who've done it before us.

Conversely, if you serve yourself first—if you give yourself permission to be selfish, to meet your own needs, and to find your own happiness—you can then give to others in the spirit of true generosity. You won't feel obligated to give. Instead, you will find that happiness is so abundant that you'll have more than enough to share.

3. **You don't need to DO anything to deserve happiness.** You don't earn it by being selfless. Nothing is required of you. Every human has the right to experience joy and love and happiness without doing anything at all to justify it. Remember Louise Hay's "Life loves you?" Well it does. You are just as worthy as the ones you're putting before yourself. You, my friend, are enough. If you feel compelled to square

up with the universe, then work on loving life right back.

4. **You're not doing anyone any favors.** Putting other people—especially your kids—before yourself tends to cripple them in some way. How will they learn to make themselves happy if you're always doing it for them? On the contrary, if you foster independence, strength, and efficacy in the people around you, they will grow. And you can do that by stepping back and allowing them to assume the roles they need to for themselves. Which gives you time for you.

Most importantly, when it comes to your kids, if you teach them that *they* deserve to be happy but *you* don't, you instill in them a sense of entitlement. And entitled teens are nothing short of assholes.

How's that for truth, my PrimeTime friend? Do you see that you don't need to be selfless? If you replace the Lie of Noble Selflessness with a giant dose of real and authentic gratitude, along with compassion for others and a belief that they can be amazingly self-reliant, you'll cuddle up in all the same warm, fuzzy feelings you used to muster from that unnecessary martyrdom. Without the resentment and anger.

Look, you shouldn't put yourself first *all* the time. But you sure as shit need to put yourself into the ball game. Learn to toss that red rubber ball back and forth. Learn to catch it as often as you throw it. Then learn to juggle it, baby.

REAL LOVE TAKES PRACTICE

Overcoming the Lie of Noble Selflessness requires practice. If you're a PrimeTime woman who has been giving herself away for decades, you might need to practice even more. What do you practice? Acts of self-love. You need to give gifts to yourself.

It's not easy to show yourself love. You might not even know how. But I'll give you a hint. Ask yourself what you would do to show your best friend love. Or your sister, your mom, or your daughter. If you wanted to show her that she was worthy, that she was valuable, that she meant the world to you, what would you do? How would you show her?

I've created a handy little list of gestures you can do for yourself to begin this practice. I recommend you try at least one per day, every single day. But before I do, let's review a few rules.

First, acts of self-love do not involve pain. Grinding through spin class is not self-love. Neither is checking off the boxes on your to-do list earlier in the day so you can run six miles after work, or suffering through a mammogram. You can certainly do those activities, but they do not fulfill the requirements of your practice. Acts of self-love feel good *while* you're doing them, not just after you're done.

Second, they cannot be conditional upon something else. You may not say, "If I stick to my diet, I'll give myself some love" or "If I finish my accounting, I'll give myself some love." You don't *do* anything to deserve love.

Once a day, do this: End the day by writing three things you did well, you admire about yourself, or you love about yourself in a "brag" journal. Talk yourself up. Compliment yourself the way you'd praise someone else. Make it a habit to say loving things to yourself and about yourself.

This may be more difficult than you think. But the more difficult it is, the more you need to practice. Many of us have no problem listening to the nasty shit we say about ourselves. But when it comes to compliments? Hell, no. If that's the case with you, then begin this nightly practice without delay!

Also, at least once a week, do one of these activities (or some other acts of your choosing) to show yourself some love:

- Buy yourself flowers.
- Buy yourself a scented candle, and light it while you read or meditate.
- Soak in a hot bath, steam bath, or hot tub, or enjoy a sauna.
- Treat yourself to a massage.
- Eat something utterly delicious.
- Watch a movie that makes you feel good.
- Read a book just for fun.
- Dress up beautifully, for no one but yourself.
- Dance wildly to your favorite song for at least five minutes.

- Take a one-hour nap.
- Do mirror work and tell yourself, "Hey, Gorgeous—I love you."
- Go somewhere you love—the coffee shop, the beach, the mall, the forest—and just *chill*.
- Watch or listen to a stand-up comedian.
- Meet your girlfriends, in person or on Skype.
- Or my all-time favorite... go to happy hour!

Are you catchin' my drift here? You can choose whatever makes you feel good. Just do it. Perform acts of self-love for no reason at all.

Once you're truly practiced, you can even love yourself when someone else is demanding something from you, because you understand that you don't *always* have to give yourself away. Can you imagine sitting in a hip little spot, sipping a martini while the eighth-grade field hockey game is in full swing? I have done this. It's a gas. Just because you don't love field hockey doesn't mean you don't love your kid or your niece. No child ever died or lost all her self-esteem because an audience wasn't readily available. In fact, learning to play for the sheer pleasure of playing is a life-changing experience for kids. I swear. I've done a ton of research.

Look, I'm not telling you to skip your kid's graduation in favor of a doobie and a Thai massage. Or to skip work once a week and watch the soaps all day. I'm just telling you to *practice*. Build these acts of self-love into your day, consciously and mindfully, until they become habits. Until you see the truth about the Lie of Noble Selflessness: You deserve to come first sometimes. Just because you're you.

EXERCISE: FINDING TIME

Many of us have entirely *unnecessary* routines that involve doing favors and chores or performing daily services for other people that we do not need to do. These are actions that others could—and likely should—do for themselves. Not doing them will NOT make us selfish, cold, or bitchy. Not doing them will NOT make people love us less, need us less, or want us less. Not doing them WILL give us time to be happier and more fulfilled. Not doing them WILL give us time to do our own, big PrimeTime thing.

Before you go to bed tonight, close your eyes and relive your entire day in your mind. Start from the moment you woke up. Watch yourself walk through the day as though you're watching a movie. Look for two red flags specifically:

1. Are you unnecessarily completing tasks that rightfully belong to other people?

2. Are you unnecessarily completing tasks that others could help you complete, if they were also contributing? (Or if you were not playing martyr, control-freak, or helicopter mom?)If so, find a way to gently transition out of these activities.

I am not suggesting that you wake up tomorrow morning and tell everyone in your house to screw off. Only that you become aware of unnecessary routines, and that you make a plan to transition out of them.

Once you have made this plan, count up the hours you will recover. Remember in Chapter 3 when I asked "What do you want?" Remember when I suggested that you make a 21-day plan for bold, decisive action toward your big source of PrimeTime pleasure? This will help you find the time for that, my friend. Find the hours. Along the way, you might also gain insight about how you're enabling or controlling or disempowering other people in your life. You might even find that your relationships are strengthened as you back off.

I'm not sure what Nancy did with the hours she gained when she stopped doing our laundry. I do know she eventually put a lock on her bedroom door. And that she hid Twizzlers and Heath Bars in there. I could hear her unwrapping them at night.

CHAPTER 10

The Lie of Irrelevance

PRIMETIME STACY

Stacy and I met on the school playground when we were seven. Each of us was wearing a different version of the same white denim outfit, featuring a silkscreened image of a man and a woman walking hand-in-hand on the beach. I can't remember if they had a dog. Nor can I remember if I wore the halter top and shorts and Stacy the crop top and bell-bottom pants, or the other way around. But in spite of our polar opposite styles, we have managed—over the past 43 years—to accidentally show up in matching outfits at no fewer than 15 events! We are like two of the Pointer Sisters, on a lifetime search for our third.

Stacy and I were popular, but never the "it" girls. We were liked well enough to be included, but left out enough to feel persecuted. By junior high, we were inseparable. As the bell sounded at the end of every period, we would search for one another in the crowded hallway, which was filled with the sounds of shrieking teens and slamming locker doors, and pass notes to each other. They were folded origami style into fat little bundles with flaps and tucks, marked with arrows and messages reading "Pull Here." In the notes, we promised to be best friends forever.

At 13, we talked our parents into letting us leave our junior high school and the crowd we found to be increasingly cruel. Stacy moved to Phoenix to live with her father, and I enrolled at a Catholic school some 15 miles away. But we still managed to spend vacations and summers together through high school and college as though we'd never been apart. By the time we'd finished college, both of us were married.

While I went off to fast-track my career in southern California, Stacy became the uber-mom to two amazing kids in an Ohio country-club community. She bought fruit snacks, and spent weekends at soccer and lacrosse tournaments. She served on charity gala boards and waited in the car line in front of private school. She moved into an enormous house, behind an enormous gate, with enormous family photos that hung above overstuffed sofas. Her lawn and her nails were immaculately manicured. She hosted slumber parties, coordinated snowboard vacations, and led school committees. She was the quintessential suburban mother and housewife. Her world was entirely unreal to me.

But then somewhere along the line, Stacy's marriage began to unravel. And by the time I had fallen madly in love with Jan and was changing Christian's diapers, she had two kids in junior high, a world of emotional hurt, and a high-dollar divorce attorney. By the time I was spending weekends at the soccer field, she was a 43-year-old, single empty nester who had never had a full-time job, trapped under the horrible Lie of Irrelevance.

To feel irrelevant is to feel disconnected. Peripheral. It is to feel, literally, beside the point. Once Stacy's marriage was over and her kids were gone, she believed she was simply extraneous. She bought into the horrible lie that she had no purpose, in and of herself. Every bit of value she had brought to the world was in relation to those around her; when they no longer needed her, devastation set in.

Unlike the Lie of Noble Selflessness, which tells us that it is moral and right to forego our needs and wants for those of others, the Lie of Irrelevance would have us believe that our *significance* is tied entirely to the roles typically played by younger women.

Night after night, we spoke on the phone, thousands of miles apart, as she worried about what she would do with herself. How would she make money? What would she do with the house? Where would she put all the stuff? How could she possibly be useful, now that her kids were gone? What value could she bring to the world? Who would even want her at this age? What skills did she have to offer?

She had lost her role. With it, she had lost her meaning.

Stacy had told herself the Lie of Irrelevance until she could tell it no more. Until she had no choice but to begin taking some sort of action. First, she packed up all her possessions and sold the house. Once she'd gained momentum through movement, she bought another house. And sold that one, too. And again. Before long, she was telling me in one of our hour-long phone calls that she'd become a bona fide Realtor.

When she invited me to her forty-seventh birthday party at her new place in the hip Short North district of Columbus, I was totally pumped. By the time my plane touched down, I was primed for martinis and mischief, and I rushed out of the gate to meet the birthday girl. She wasn't there. Instead, I had a text message telling me to meet her at the curb.

I barely recognized her. She stood next to her massive Lexus SUV in a tailored navy blazer, pressed white blouse, and leather riding boots. She wore an expression of determination and concentration that she had never donned in my presence. She looked up from the phone and silently mouthed, "I have to take this call." I rode away from the airport alongside a Stacy I had never imagined.

She was negotiating over the phone. And she was as tough as fucking nails. Stacy, who had avoided confrontation her whole life. Stacy, who had lamented daily about what she would do with herself. Stacy was telling other people what to do with themselves. And they were listening.

She discussed contingencies and multiple offers. She told her buyer to calm down and wait. She told the seller's agent that she'd better get her client in line. She demanded information about inspections, and made it clear that she would accept nothing less than what she and her client had already stipulated. Again, she talked her client down from the ledge. At least three times, she found a wholly professional but entirely unmistakable way of telling someone to go fuck themselves.

As we rolled up to a stoplight, I looked over and asked, "Who ARE you?"

Over the course of the weekend, between martinis and shoe shopping, bar hopping and tapas, chick flicks and laughing fits, Stacy sold two houses. She walked around with a phone to one ear and a finger in the other, so she could hear over the background noise. She had file folders in her back seat. She emailed documents from her phone. She reassured everyone, in no uncertain terms, that everything would be just fine. And I believed every word she said. She was so completely in charge that I was ready to make an offer. She stunned the living shit out of me.

Within the next two years, my friend Stacy—who had just recently felt entirely irrelevant in her own mind—became a hotshot at high-dollar home sales. She sold millions of dollars in real estate, and she built a brand for herself that was airtight and based on serious talent and no-nonsense communication. Then she packed up what was left of her stuff, and she headed out to Cali. For the first time since we were 13, she now lives right down the street.

Last year at the age of 50, Stacy landed her dream job. She no longer sells houses. She now sells franchises to real estate brokers for one of the top real estate conglomerates in the world. She's so fucking useful and powerful that I can hardly stand it. She is PrimeTime to the max. Because she stopped leaning on the Lie of Irrelevance, and decided to make a life for herself. She stopped looking outside of herself for a purpose, and reached deep inside to find potential.

YOU'RE MISSING THE POINT

Let me make it crystal clear that I am in no way insinuating that the transition into PrimeTime is "all in your head." This shift is 100% real. I'm sure the 48 million women who are presently in menopause will be happy to back me up on that. Biologically, this is the most significant shift we'll experience since puberty. This is fucking substantial, my friend.

Feelings of irrelevance will likely seize most every PrimeTime woman at some point, because prior to midlife it's quite common for us to tie our identities to relationships. We learn to associate our esteem with our marriage, our home, our kids. The shifts in these relationships can be monumental, giving tremendous power to this lie.

But we PrimeTime women feel irrelevant about far more than just our kids. In fact, you don't need to be a mom at all to have these feelings. We feel irrelevant as our physical bodies age. We feel irrelevant as younger women enter the workforce. We feel irrelevant as the men around us grapple with their own midlife transitions. We feel irrelevant as we struggle to redefine "sexy." We feel irrelevant as technology advances and we rush to keep up.

Believe me when I tell you that the train has *not* left the station. You can overcome those feelings. But you have to make a choice. You can either dwindle, diminish, and shrink as you languish in the gap between what was and what could be. Or you can expand, my beautiful friend. You can blow this shit UP! You can approach midlife as a time of loss, or you can jump into PrimeTime and grab everything there is. You must choose.

You are not irrelevant. This is YOUR fucking PrimeTime. You ARE the point! But you need to realize your own Prime-Time significance. And you make that shift in two ways:

- What you do
- What you say

JUST DO IT

Irrelevant is a pretty shitty way to feel. It's a self-esteem crusher. One of the fundamental building blocks of self-esteem is efficacy, our ability to make things happen. Climbing out from under the Lie of Irrelevance is all about taking action. When we act, we prove to ourselves that we can produce results… which increases our confidence to take more action… which further enhances our sense of self-worth.

When you wallow or mope or sit around thinking about what you've lost, you'll also lose momentum. Remember in the Rage Triathlon when I fell over on my bicycle? That was all about lack of momentum. Pedaling uphill from a dead stop is a serious fucking struggle. Motion begets motion. So start pedaling. Right now. Do not stop.

Action and momentum were everything for Stacy. With every small action she took—packing a box, selling her house, taking the real estate exam, moving cross-country—she validated her ability to produce a result. She repeatedly went through trial and course correction, trial and course correction. As she gained momentum, she also gained a new sense of self. She no longer needed someone else to need her for her to feel valued and purposeful. And she started having a great time in the process.

This is why I preached so long and so hard about finding your big PrimeTime pursuit. If you define and visualize what you want—and you take action toward achieving it—the Lie of Irrelevance will show itself for exactly what it is: total bullshit. You are not less relevant because you are in midlife. You *feel* less relevant because you stopped *doing* something that made you feel important. So do something else, for Christ's sake! But this time, do it for you.

What I saw with so many PrimeTime women as I prepared for this book was the senseless belief that midlife must be a time of loss. With that belief comes a tendency to cling. We cling to the way our lives, our marriages, our relationships with our kids, or our bodies *used* to be. We cling to the way things can no longer be. We do this because we lack imagination about the way life *could* be.

With every action you take, you will ignite your imagination. You will open yourself up to possibilities. You will empower yourself through momentum. You will, through action, facilitate more opportunity.

Here's what I like about *doing* things (as opposed to thinking, worrying, planning, analyzing, or lamenting). Not only will action enhance your self-esteem and boost your confidence, it will also put you on a path toward adventure. You don't need to earn a degree in civil engineering or enter a robotics competition. Just apply yourself to what you *want*. Make yourself useful to *you*. And the world will open up before you.

Let me tell you about another serious boon in all of this. The relationships you're so worried about losing—the ones with your kids who are leaving home, your spouse who may also be experiencing a shift, your colleagues at work, or even your own body—will be infused with a new kind of passion. You won't feel needy or clingy. On the contrary, my friend! You will be stimulated. You will be aroused. You will be fired up. You will be fucking PrimeTime in motion! And everyone you know and meet will feel it.

PrimeTime women told me they had four primary concerns as they approached the age of 50.

1. What will I do with myself when my kids are gone?
2. What will my husband/partner and I talk about when the kids are gone?
3. How can I keep my love relationship interesting in the bedroom?
4. What will I do about my aging body?

Every one of these concerns is about remaining relevant. Significant. Important. And every one of them is best addressed through action.

If you want to fill in the space when your kids are gone, then find something meaningful to do for yourself. Nothing is more entertaining than living out your own potential.

If you want something to talk about with your partner—or if you want to find a partner who thinks you're fascinating—then find something exciting to do. Nothing is more interesting than adventure.

If you want to waltz into the bedroom and know that you're a stone-cold fox, then find something courageous to do. Nothing is sexier than confidence and self-assurance.

And if you want to keep your aging body in shape, then find something active to do. Nothing will make your body work better than moving it around and finding out just what it's capable of.

If you're falling victim to the Lie of Irrelevance, I have one question for you: What the fuck are you gonna DO about it?

SAY THIS TO LIFE

I realize that it's not always easy to take that first step. What if you're stuck in the gap? What if you've already lost momentum? What if you're terrified as hell? What if you feel you're your motivation has been lost? What if you don't even know what the first step is?

Then focus on a single, powerful word: YES.

The biggest shift I saw in Stacy—the one that put her back in the driver's seat—was a shift to saying yes to whatever came her way. At first, she just said yes to the suggestions that she should do *something*. She said yes to packing the first box. And she started saying it every day.

Now, seven years later, Stacy says yes more than anyone I know. She says yes to travel, to new restaurants, to weekend getaways, to life changes that her kids are going through. She says yes to meetups with new women and to music festivals. She says yes to a glass of Pinot Gris on my patio and dancing with me to Funk Radio on Pandora. She says yes to lasagna and chick flicks. She says yes to all kinds of new physical stuff like yoga and hikes and barre class. Every time I talk to her, she's checking out something new. With every yes, her imagination expands regarding what her PrimeTime can be.

You must realize something, however. In the beginning, you must create the opportunities for yes. You can't just sit around the house waiting for an offer. Check the local paper or the internet. Walk into the new sushi joint down the street or go to the movies on your own. Reach out to another PrimeTime woman who would love to enjoy this shit with you.

If you want to feel relevant, if you want to own your power, if you want to rock the next 30 years like you rocked the last 40 or 50, start saying "Yes!"

And listen up, because this is a gem. If you have a transition coming up—if your kids will be moving out in the next few years, or you're headed toward retirement, or you're nearing the time when you'll be charged with the care for your own aging parents—then start saying yes *before* the transition. Don't wait until you're lost in the gap. Don't come to a screeching halt, like my beautiful friend Stacy did. Because momentum is everything.

If you start pedaling up that hill now, you'll be flying down the other side before you know it, with the wind in your hair, screaming "FUCK YEAH!" at the top of your lungs.

SAY THIS TO YOURSELF

The last part of seeing through the Lie of Irrelevance is about what you say to *yourself*. While saying yes to life is critical for facilitating action, and taking action is vital for feeling confident and capable, you must also recognize a fundamental universal *truth* in order to see the Lie of Irrelevance for the bullshit that it truly is.

The truth? You do not need to DO anything at all to be worthy and valuable. You were *born* worthy and valuable. You are enough, just as you are. Your worth is not *contingent*; it is *inherent*. It is not about your behavior; it is about your existence. It is about self-acceptance. And it might not be as difficult as you think.

You accept your inherent worth simply by saying:

I am I, I exist, and I am alive.

I have studied, and incorporated into my daily life, a powerful but easy practice for living in truth, instead of living inside the Lies that Bind. It requires practice, because it's not natural to see the truth when we've been lying our whole lives. Living in truth requires us to find—and remain in—a certain frame of mind. A mantra practice is a seriously powerful tool for establishing mindset.

A mantra will help you maintain a connection to the state you want to cultivate. To reverse the Lie of Irrelevance, that state is one where you feel perfectly free to pursue your big PrimeTime thing. It's a state where you feel comfortable seeking out your own joy. Where you do not need to explain or excuse yourself for meeting your own needs and chasing after your dreams. Where you know that you are absolutely worthy of a life fulfilled.

Mantras are the basis for almost every spiritual practice. A mantra is simply a string of words that are repeated over and over. They may be spoken, sung, or chanted. They are said to have intense healing powers, because they help you access deeper levels of consciousness. The right mantra will guide you to a place inside yourself where you will seriously dig hanging out.

This may seem like ridiculous, woo-woo crap to you. I get that. I really do. But trust me when I tell you that there is nothing remotely ridiculous about learning to tell yourself the truth. If you're anything like me and the rest of the Prime-Time women I've featured in this book, then for the past 40 or 50 years, you've been telling yourself some preposterous lies. So why not give the truth a shot?

Here's the best part about a mantra. You don't need to believe it for it to have power. Over time, it will take you to the place where you know your inherent worth, regardless of your resistance. It will take you to the still, small place inside you that already knew the truth, before life covered it up. It will override those thoughts that would have you believe you must accomplish something, serve someone, fulfill a role, or make something happen in order to be significant. A mantra knows that MY THOUGHTS = BULLSHIT. A mantra is the whole package, baby.

You can repeat your mantra when you're meditating (instead of saying "SO/HUM"), you can use it when you're doing yoga, or you can say it all damn day long. You can speak it out loud or quietly in your mind. You can chant it to yourself when you're running or cycling or doing Zumba. Pull it out and put it to work any time you'd like. Just say it over and over again.

Choose any of these phrases as your mantra, or invent your own:

- I am I, I exist, and I am alive.
- I am worthy.
- I am worth it all.
- Life loves me.
- The world (or God, if you prefer) is on my side.
- May I be happy and free.

The Lie of Irrelevance is dangerous, because it causes us to cling to the past. We will never remain relevant by looking back or by grasping at what once was. We will remain relevant by moving forward. By experiencing. By endeavoring. By living.

You cannot have what you once had. But this is Prime-Time, baby. You can have something so much better.

****

Back when Nancy was still doing my laundry, she emptied my pants pockets each day and found those notes that Stacy and I had passed in the hallways. She carefully unfolded them and stored them in a box in the laundry room. When I was in my 30s, she gave them back to me, along with the journals I'd left in my bedroom when I had moved out.

A few months ago, Stacy and I poured a couple glasses of wine, pulled out those notes and journals, and traveled back in time. We relived all the nonsense we'd gotten up to as kids. The boys we'd kissed at the roller skating rink and the girls we'd argued with at the school dances. The fights we'd had with our moms and the teachers who we'd thought were lame and unfair. We remembered the silly insecurities and the senseless self-recrimination. The struggles to fit in and the yearning to be liked. But mostly, we remembered how we'd wished that we were older, so we could do whatever we wanted and show the world we were not to be fucked with.

Then we laughed like hell. Because that's just what we're doing now.

CHAPTER 11

The Lie of Extenuating Circumstances

FRAGILE—THIS END UP

At my Catholic high school, I was the only girl in my grade with divorced parents. I was also the only one who, every now and then, showed up at school in a rusted Delta 88 driven by a 24-year-old brother who was smoking a joint and listening to ZZ Top. I was the only one interested in sex before the eleventh grade. The only one who swore. And the only one who lived in a little farm town 10 miles from school.

I was the odd girl out. From the wrong side of the tracks. A complete stranger to the social set I struggled to belong to. No matter how official my burgundy jumper, knee socks, and penny loafers looked, they did not entitle me to be part of the upper-crust college-prep crowd.

Confronted daily by the wacky pandemonium of our family life and the wildly conflicting lessons in Catholic doctrine that told me how sinful I was, I became afraid to speak my own truth and distrustful of my own voice. So I retreated to the world inside my head. Which was unfortunate, because it was a shit show in there.

By the time I was fully through puberty, I'd developed thought patterns so illogical and destructive that I ricocheted from one self-created chaos to another like a pinball. By the end of freshman year, I was having private sessions with a therapist. She was a wonderfully smart and brutally honest Jewish mother who genuinely understood me. But she could not save me from myself—or from what I thought of myself.

At 16, I hooked up with an abusive boyfriend. At 17, I attempted suicide, and spent 6 weeks of my senior year in the psychiatric ward at the local hospital. For a girl my age, these were self-defining choices. And they substantiated a label that I wore, both privately and publicly, for years to come: FRAGILE.

I developed a rich internal dialogue that supported this label. I was quick to tell myself exaggerations or untruths like "I can't cope with this" or "I can't take it anymore" or "This is all too much for me." I often entertained the thought "I'm totally falling apart." Although I ultimately righted my situation and my sense of self-worth, the label took on a life of its own, and long outlived my actual dysfunction.

In stark contrast to the emotional delicacy I ascribed to myself, I was a solid performer. I aced undergrad school, worked my way up to vice president status by 24, and thrived in the MBA for Executives program, despite the fact that they initially denied me entry because I was too young. I was a solid earner, a strategic thinker, and an effective leader.

I never said no to an opportunity for advancement, and I never doubted that I could nail any task. I just had serious qualms about whether I was up for the struggle. Rarely did I hold my own feet to the fire where serious effort or hardship were concerned. Because I was special—competent, but FRAGILE.

After Jan and I moved into our first tiny apartment together, I came to understand the Lie of Extenuating Circumstances. On the day my lie was exposed, we were having an especially volatile argument. I had received a collections notice for a loan I'd decided I was too delicate to pay.

Because I was a horrible victim of my own decisions (and my own labels), I'd created a massive financial mess in my 20s. In this instance, I had been feeling harassed and mistreated by the lending institution I'd shafted. Their collection methods, in my opinion, were downright rude. They lacked compassion.

On a gorgeous, sunny Saturday morning, their final collections notice—the one that threated a lawsuit—arrived in the mail. I watched Jan open it and fall down (more than sit down) onto our yellow-and-white-striped IKEA futon, as though someone had knocked the wind out of him. As his eyes scanned the letter, I watched his anger rise. When he finished, he glared at me with absolute fury and scorn.

He shouted and railed at me for the mess I'd created but had refused to clean up. I was both ashamed and utterly indignant. So I did what I did best at that time in my life. I cried. I curled up into a ball, assumed my FRAGILE stance, and sobbed. (If I'm being totally honest here, I may have even crawled under a desk for dramatic effect.)

I told him that I couldn't take it. That I was special, and that he was mean. That Bank of Whatever had no idea what I had been through. That *he* had no idea what I had been through. That my divorce had been terribly tough, and I needed a fresh start. That life was just too damn difficult for someone as emotionally sensitive as me.

Then he bent over and looked me in the eye and said something I have never forgotten—not for a single day—since he uttered it nearly 20 years ago.

"Julie, I love you. But the only thing wrong with you is that you *think* there's something wrong with you."

WHAAAT? What a horrible thing to say!

Of *course*, there was something wrong with me! I had a *sickness*! Anyone who looked at me could plainly see it!

But in that moment, the jig was up. The Lie of Extenuating Circumstances was exposed. And so was I. In an entirely rare moment, I was rendered speechless.

Then he said something that snapped me out of my self-imposed misery and into a place of action. He told me that my refusal to own my potential was the greatest waste of talent he had ever witnessed. And he said, "Julie, I will walk to edge of the cliff with you, but I will not jump off. If you want to be in a relationship with me, you need to clean this shit up."

I did. I *intended* to be in a relationship with him for the rest of my life. So I cleaned my shit up.

In the weeks and months that followed, I began to clearly see—for the first time—how I had used my FRAGILE label to weasel my way out of so many difficult predicaments that I was fully equipped to handle. How I had avoided my own potential, in favor of pity and support, and how I had justified it all with a single action I'd taken nearly 15 years earlier.

It took me several long years to pay back the debt I had amassed. But I paid back every penny. It also took me several years to ditch the crutch. But eventually I became a trained professional at recognizing the Lie of Extenuating Circumstances and eradicating it from my life.

I stopped telling myself that I was different. That something was broken in me and needed to be fixed. That I deserved a pass. That my circumstances were special, because I had been mistreated, unloved, and forgotten. I stopped telling myself that being FRAGILE was a legitimate excuse to consistently operate below my own potential.

At first, I had to practice. I'd play out my bullshit the way I'd always played it, and see the pity party in hindsight. After a while, I'd catch myself in the act, and I would stop myself right in the middle of the party. Eventually, I was able to see it coming and replace the pity party (before the balloons and the DJ arrived) with the truth.

Our circumstances do not prevent us from experiencing happiness or success. But our reactions to those circumstances, and the labels we create for ourselves, most certainly do.

I learned one more crucial aspect of this lie along the way. We don't use this lie *just* to avoid what we dislike. We also use it to avoid taking chances. We use it to sidestep our own greatness. We use it to stay small.

I learned that *in every moment*, we have a choice: We can step forward into possibility, or we can step backward into the comfort of certainty.

And more often than not, we choose comfort and certainty. Even if it means misery.

THE CIRCUMSTANCES OF PRIMETIME

Not everyone tells this lie to the extreme that I did. The PrimeTime women I met, interviewed, coached, and led over the past few years were not FRAGILE or wallowing in self-pity. But every one of them told the Lie of Extenuating Circumstances in some form when it came to explaining why she wasn't doing her big PrimeTime thing. Every woman had a *reason* that her desire wasn't her reality.

They told me they would never find love because they were too old. Women insisted they couldn't succeed in business because they had too much on their plates. I heard excuses like these:

- I'm too distracted.
- My dad never approved.

- I'm bad at math.
- I've always been overweight.
- I'm broke.
- I can't speak in public.
- My husband drinks too much.
- I drink too much.
- My aging parents are too demanding.
- My kids need special care.
- My hormones are out of balance.
- I'm making too much money doing *this* to take a chance on *that*.

The Lie of Extenuating Circumstances is a tricky one, because it comes in so many different models. Often when we tell this lie we don't talk about how hard we have it. Instead, we talk about how good someone else has it.

We say:

- That's easy for her.
- She's lucky.
- I could write a better book than that, if only…
- I could do that too, if I weren't burdened with…

Sometimes we use the lie to define ourselves.
We say:

- I'm the kind of person who…

- I have a blah, blah, blah personality.
- I've never been one to…
- I'm just not that kind of girl.

No matter what model we choose for the Lie of Extenuating Circumstances, underneath it lives a LABEL that we've created. That label is based on one of two beliefs.

1. Something is wrong with *me* that I must fix before I can nail this.

   OR

2. Something special about my *situation* prevents me from living out my dream.

Either way you slice it, it's bullshit.

It may be bullshit that you've always told yourself. It may be bullshit that someone else has always told you about yourself. It may even be based on a foundational truth. But trust me. It's bullshit, nonetheless.

LABEL MAKING 101

I had the divine pleasure to attend a series of coaching sessions with Dr. Adi Jaffe. He is a professor at UCLA who did a TEDx talk called "Rebranding Our Shame." In it, he speaks about the labels we place upon ourselves, and how we allow those labels to cripple us. Dr. Jaffe's talk is about mental health issues, specifically. But his discussion about labels applies to any name we call ourselves or any affliction we use to describe ourselves, as well as any label we use to *avoid* taking action.

In the talk, Dr. Jaffe says we learn to believe that "a certain label comes with a specific amount of dysfunction." And that all sense of nuance is removed when we brand ourselves in this way. It becomes an all-or-nothing game. We give in to a concept (the concept associated with the label) and forget that we're individuals, and that nothing about us or our lives is black-and-white.

Dr. Jaffe mentions a study that shows the power of labels. At the beginning of a school year, a class of elementary school children in California were chosen to complete a series of tests. One of them was The Harvard Test of Inflected Acquisition. The teachers were told to expect great things from a specific group of kids who had apparently scored a certain way on this test. At the end of the year, when the kids completed a battery of follow-up tests, the ones who had been singled out for greatness had indeed increased their IQ scores by as many as 15 points more than the other students.

In truth, The Harvard Test of Inflected Acquisition was a total farce. The students who were "destined for greatness" had been chosen completely at random. But the teachers—*acting* on a false belief based on this label—*caused* the increase in their IQ scores by providing them with extra attention. And by doing so, they let some of the other kids fall behind.

This is an extreme example. But it's pertinent to our lives. And to the Lie of Extenuating Circumstances. Yet in reality, the situation generally works in *reverse*. We use this lie to *limit* our actions.

How many names do you call yourself? How many ways do you label your situations? How many "afflictions" do you ascribe to your health, your personality, your career viability, your marriage, your kids, or your family members?

Pay close attention to any qualities you believe you possess too much of, or not enough of. Are you too old, too fat, too shy, too weak, too late, too dumb, too inexperienced, or too disorganized? Are you not strong enough, brave enough, sharp enough, balanced enough, or self-controlled enough?

Also, be exceptionally careful of the things in your life that you think you hold too much of (responsibility, trouble, chaos, family, bills, fear, health issues, demanding people) or not enough of (money, time, opportunity, support, freedom, education). "Too" and "not enough" are hallmarks of the Lie of Extenuating Circumstances.

How many painful, shameful moments from your past do you carry around with you like weights on your back? How many experiences are you using to define yourself? And most importantly, how many times do you *use* these as limitations or excuses to avoid the work that's required for you to grab hold of what you truly desire?

I'm about to say something that might make you gasp. It might make you throw this book down, stomp out of the room, and call me a nasty name. But I gotta say it.

You are not special. You are just like everyone else. No set of extenuating circumstances gives you a pass on living out your destiny or pursuing your maximum potential.

As my good friend George Bernard Shaw said, "People always blame their circumstances for what they are. I don't believe in circumstances. The people who get on in the world are the people who get up and look for the circumstances they want, and if they can't find them, make them."

I need to tell you something else. Nothing is wrong with you that needs to be fixed. The only thing wrong with you is that you think there's something wrong with you. You are absolutely 100% enough. Just as you are.

So it's time to drop the label, baby. It's time to shift the way you see and use the circumstances that you think make you special. It's time to make the world your own in PrimeTime.

Here's what you must understand about this lie: It's not the LABEL that's the lie, it's the belief that the label *prevents* us from doing what we want that's the lie. It's the use of the label as an excuse or a story to avoid our big, hairy, scary PrimeTime goal that's the lie.

The Lie of Extenuating Circumstances doesn't only come about in PrimeTime. We tell ourselves this lie our whole lives. But it is especially *pertinent* in PrimeTime for several reasons.

- In PrimeTime, we come to recognize unfinished business from when we were young. We're faced with the reality that it's now or never. With those dreams from the past come the insecurities and labels of the past. With the desire comes the potential pain of pursuit. And with potential pain comes excuses to avoid it.

- On the flip side, many of us are presented with MORE time during PrimeTime, based on shifts in responsibility. Our kids are leaving the house, we're approaching retirement, our spouses are retiring and pitching in, or any number of transitions. With this time comes opportunity. And with that opportunity comes fear and resistance. With fear and resistance come excuses.
- The other five Lies that Bind become part of our narrative. "Midlife" becomes part of our label. We're "special" because we're *less than* what we once were. In the ultimate irony, we use the fact that we're middle-aged to avoid pursuing what we desire in middle age. It's utter nonsense, my friend.

I've told you that it's my mission to rebrand PrimeTime. If you're like most of the incredibly viable, capable, and remarkable PrimeTime women I've worked with, you may need to do a little rebranding work on yourself too. If you want to rock this bitch, you've gotta lay down the labels and stop using your circumstances as an excuse.

CIRCUMSTANTIAL EVIDENCE

The way out of this lie is simple. It's not easy, but it's totally straightforward. You need to watch your thoughts. Just like I mentioned in Mad Girl Math. Watch your thoughts float by like clouds, and see where your bullshit labels and stories lie. When you *don't* take action, what is it that you're telling yourself? When you stay stuck in the status quo, what's your reason? When you dance *around* whatever you told yourself you wanted in the mirror, what is it that's stopping you from making it yours?

Find these self-limiting labels and stories. And find them fast.

Then tell yourself the truth. For every label, every circumstance, every challenge, every supposed shortcoming you face, someone else in the world faces that same challenge TIMES 10 and still works for what she desires. Tell yourself the truth. *I am not special.* Then give yourself a fucking chance by taking *action.*

I talked about action in the last chapter. And there will be a whole lot more of it in the chapters to come. But first, let's shed some serious light on another practice that will help with the Lie of Extenuating Circumstances.

It's gratitude.

Gratitude is a state of being. To be grateful is to be appreciative, thankful, and content with what we have. But trust me when I say that this also requires practice. Those of us who believe the Lie of Extenuating Circumstances have lived in a state of lack. We have operated from a position of "not enough." We have focused on what we don't have, or what we need, rather than what we've been given. To shift that focus, we must practice. Every single day.

A gratitude practice will do a lot more than shift your thinking. It will bring you joy. It will provide you with an overwhelming sense that everything will be okay. It will improve your relationships and increase the chances that cool people will dig hanging out with you. And it will put an end to the excuses that are born from a feeling of lack.

I recommend two gratitude practices to my clients. I have used them both, and found them easy, effective, and even fun.

Gratitude Jar: Find yourself a nice big, clear jar, jug, vase, or fishbowl and a little notepad. Put it somewhere you walk past several times each day. The kitchen counter is an excellent spot for a gratitude jar.

Each time you see it, grab that notepad and write down something—anything—for which you are grateful. It might be a single word, like "sunshine." Or you might write, "My son gave me a kiss today for the first time in forever." It might be the ripe peach you just ate, or the fact that you're having an excellent hair day. Just write it down. Then fold that sucker up into a tiny little square and toss it into the jar.

You can invite the rest of your family members too. You can even make it available to visitors in your home. The joy is in watching the jar fill up. As you move forward with this daily practice, *you* will become filled with gratitude as the jar fills. And the way you see your circumstances will begin to shift.

Then choose a point in time. (Some people do this when they're feeling low, others do it on a special day like New Year's Day.) Dump out that jar. Take the time to read all those little pieces of paper. Relive those grateful moments. Relish the memories. Then start the process anew.

Gratitude Journal: Each night before you go to bed, write down three things for which you are grateful. Don't feel pressured to be wildly inventive or creative. Don't explain why or compose big paragraphs. Just three quick things you're grateful for. In the morning when you wake up, do it again. (By the way, this practice will be especially easy if you've already started a Brag Journal to show yourself some love. Just add your gratitude right into that journal.)

When you begin and end your days with abundance—with a focus on what you HAVE rather than what you have NOT—you will begin to shift. The bullshit stories you're carrying around will begin to lose their strength and importance. Eventually, you will see them for exactly what they are: Lies of Extenuating Circumstances.

****

In 2014, I flew to Columbus for my 30-year class reunion, and I stayed at Stacy's house for the weekend. I'd stressed for weeks about what I would wear and what I would say. I got all worked up about the opinions of people I had not spoken to in more than a quarter century.

As I walked into the shadowy, wood-paneled barroom of a conservative Ohio country club, every self-doubt and insecurity I'd felt as a 16-year-old girl from the wrong side of the tracks washed over me. I played with my long, red, curly bangs in an attempt to cover the FRAGILE that was written right across my forehead.

But I smiled and hugged and shook hands. I relived a thousand memories and reminisced with stories from back in the day. I had several drinks too many. When I got back to Stacy's house at the end of the night, I threw up right on her front lawn. Just like the irresponsible, out-of-control girl I once had once been.

I had completely forgotten the power of that FRAGILE label. The sway it held over me. The way it weakened me, diminished me, and held me down. It hit me like seven shots of vodka.

The next day, over champagne brunch, I filled Stacy in on what I could remember. We had more than a few laughs. I peeled off that FRAGILE label and stuck GRATEFUL in its place. I was grateful that the night had shown me how far I'd come. Grateful that I no longer felt a yearning to be accepted by a crowd. Grateful that I was loved, in love, and loving my life. And especially grateful that I'd made it to the front yard before I'd let it rip.

CHAPTER 12

The Lie of the Empty Hourglass

PRIME TIME CARLA

On a scorching hot August night in Arizona, my friend Carla and I climbed into an enormous four-poster bed next to her mother, Pauline. It would prove to be one of Pauline's last nights on Earth. As Carla and I lay with her under the covers, we held her hands and talked to her about girl stuff.

We talked to her as though nothing had changed. As though she'd never been ravaged by breast cancer. As though she had never shopped for wigs or seen attorneys about the state of her affairs. As though the 15 bottles of pills on her nightstand didn't exist. As though we were having a girl party in a swanky Las Vegas hotel room, like we'd done so many times before. We told her stories and jokes. We kissed her ever-so-gently, and we looked at one another knowingly as she drifted off to sleep.

Later, Carla and I sat for hours in the colossal kitchen that Pauline had designed. Among the slabs of granite, the travertine tiles, the cherry-wood cabinets with stainless steel hardware, the side-by-side refrigerator, the blown-glass vases, and the amber jars filled with dried pasta, we sat and we cried. And we whispered about what Carla would do.

Carla had moved into the house to care for Pauline in her final weeks. The move had been a short one. Only 10 houses separated Pauline's from the one down the street that Carla had formerly shared with her own husband. Ten ranch-style homes with beautifully manicured front lawns and backyards with swimming pools that faced the tenth fairway of a perfectly landscaped country-club course. But down that stretch of street, no more than a quarter mile, Carla had taken the longest journey of her life.

After nearly 25 years of marriage, she had walked away from a man she'd once loved madly and fiercely. Only months earlier, when the restaurant she'd painstakingly built with her bare hands was filled with nothing but empty chairs, she'd been forced to walk away from that too. The recession of 2008 had pillaged and plundered. While the street she lived on looked as lavish as ever, behind the giant, maple front doors and etched windows lived many other couples who'd also been withered and ruined by forces they could not control.

We had shoved Carla's clothes, shoes, toiletries, and most important personal possessions into thick, black lawn-and-garden trash bags and carried them down the street to

Pauline's. They were bulky and heavy. But it was the weight of Carla's situation that had made us sweat and cry.

It was only natural that Carla would walk to Pauline; they had a mother-daughter partnership like none I've seen before or since. Together, they sparkled. The best-dressed pair at any party, they taught me that leopard print goes with everything and nothing, and that only a hint of it is required. That a life without fancy is a life without fun. And that even the girliest of girls can be the most formidable of forces. They taught me to be glamorous.

With Pauline, we always drank champagne, Veuve Clicquot. We drank from long-stemmed glasses that were bejeweled and engraved and had been perfectly chilled in the freezer. After her eyes had been destroyed by macular degeneration and she could see only the vaguest of shapes, she would hear my voice when I entered a room and say, "Is that my Julie? Should we have a glass of champagne?"

Once the blindness set in, Carla rearranged Pauline's legendary closet—tops on the top bar, bottoms on the bottom—into perfectly coordinated sections divided by heavy plastic trash bags that Pauline could reach out and feel. She could blindly choose any top, bottom, shoe, belt, and handbag from within a section, and put together a smashing outfit. She may not have been able to see us, but we could certainly still see her.

She would toss her head back and laugh, the shiny strands of her beautiful chestnut hair sliding back to uncover her left eye, her long, thin fingers wrapped around the stem of the champagne glass. She would say, "You girls!" And we would giggle along with her.

Pauline's battle with cancer was the second one that this dynamic mother-daughter duo had endured. When Carla was 14, she'd had ovarian cancer herself. Even after a complete hysterectomy, her chances for survival were slim. But thanks to a doctor who was willing to conduct aggressive experimental treatments, Carla had pulled through.

When we were packing her belongings for the move, she pulled out a book that her doctor had written after her recovery. For the first time, I saw a full-page, sepia-toned photo of a pre-pubescent Carla, completely bald from the chemo treatments. She looked like an imp, a stunning little sprite. But as sick as she was, her eyes told the world in no uncertain terms that she would not be discounted. She would not be written off.

I'd fallen in love with that look when I'd first met Carla. I was 17 and she was 24 when she'd married my dad's best friend. I'd followed that look in her eyes to parties, dinners, weekend road trips, and day-long shopping adventures for decades afterward. That look had always told me that not only would everything be alright, it would be big fucking fun.

But that night, as we whispered in the kitchen, that look was gone. It had been replaced by a look of complete and utter despair. Once Pauline was gone, Carla would have nowhere to live. She had little money and even less energy. But that wasn't what worried her the most.

As I stared into eyes I had never seen before, I assured her, "Carla, you cannot see this now, but there will be a time when all of this will pass. There will be a time when you will be happy again."

She shook her head and forced a defeated smile. "I'm not getting any younger, Juls," she said as she sighed. "I can't even imagine that. There just isn't enough time left."

Ahh, the lie. The Lie of the Empty Hourglass.

HOUR AFTER HOUR

Listen to me when I tell you this. Unless what you want for PrimeTime is to compete in the 1984 Olympics, you still have time.

- At 57, Peggy Whitson became the oldest woman to blast off into space. Then 534 days later, she surpassed Jeff Williams' record as the longest-serving American in space. As I write this, she's still out there.
- At 94, Iris Apfel was the inspiration for a line of MAC cosmetics.
- Joan Rivers was the first woman to host a late-night talk show. She landed the gig at 53.
- Dr. Ruth Westheimer first became the go-to girl for all things sexual in her mid-50s, when she launched her hit radio show, *Sexually Speaking*.
- Carla opened a new business at 52. And she's fucking crushing it today.

You are not out of time. You are perfectly on time. You are stunningly, powerfully, wonderfully PrimeTime.

Let's do some math, since we've gotten so good at it together. This math will show you the truth.

Truth #1: The amazing Bill Gates said, "We always overestimate the change that will occur in the next two years and underestimate the change that will occur in the next ten. Don't let yourself be lulled into inaction." If you're in PrimeTime—and we know that the average life expectancy for women is 81 (and by no means are you average)—then you've got that 10 years, my friend. You've got that 10 years, many times over! Keep that in mind as you create a plan for what you want.

Truth #2: Research shows that you can become competent at something—meaning you can figure it out well enough to do it and enjoy it—after about 50 hours of practice. Whether you want to golf, become a blogger, bake pastries, begin an online business, learn fencing, or speak fluent Japanese, you can complete about 50 hours of training in just about anything, and it will start to become fun. It takes just 50 hours to change your life.

"Seriously, Juju—50 hours?" you ask. "How the hell can I change my life in 50 hours?"

Let me give you an example that will ring the bell for you. This week, my son, Christian—the one who had climbed out the window into a rainstorm less than three years ago—slid into the driver's seat of my car. He had just obtained his learner's permit. You have not truly come face to face with the potential for your own demise until you've taken a ride in a car with a fifteen-year-old boy. It is absolutely terrifying.

The California DMV requires that drivers under the age of 17½ hold their learner's permits—and drive with consenting adults—for 6 months before they can receive their licenses. During that time, they must complete 50 hours behind the wheel.

Those 50 hours dramatically alter the life of every teenager—and every parent—who experience them. Set aside the fact that I lie in bed every night catching my breath and willing my blood pressure to drop and my heartbeat to slow, as though I've just been chased by a lion across the savanna. And think for a moment about some larger implications of those 50 hours. Think about how the world will open up for Christian once he can drive. Think about the adventures he will have. The freedom he will enjoy. The confidence he will gain. The moments of unadulterated "Fuck you...this is aaaall mine" that he will experience.

Think about the fact that my days of carpooling have come to an end.

If this boy can learn to drive a motor vehicle in 50 hours, over 6 months, what can you do in the same amount of time?

Truth #3: This last truth is for the overachievers in the group. As convention would have it, it takes 10,000 hours to become an expert at something. Expert. Top notch. A pro. A leader. A competitor. An authority. A baller. In 10,000 hours, you can rule the fucking world. If you worked at something full-time, 10,000 hours would take about 5 years.

I'm quite certain that when you gave up the Lie of Noble Selflessness, you found yourself some additional hours. Even if you only find yourself an hour a week, that means that in a year—52 total hours—you'll be doing something you've never done, and lovin' it. You'll be on it, my friend. You'll be snowboarding. Or knitting. Or practicing your TED talk in front of a local women's group. But in order to finish the 50 hours, you must begin them.

Imagine what it will be like when you're actually *doing* what you dreamt of, and you're good at it. Imagine what it will feel like as you enjoy it while heading toward expert status. Imagine what it will be like—as your friends suffer through empty nest syndrome and cry in their coffee—when you're laughing your ass off with a glass of Pinot Noir in hand, because you just sold your first watercolor painting of a Boston Terrier for 500 large.

If you're not convinced, then get a load of this. After Stuart Grauer challenged me to find something to do, I decided to start my big PrimeTime push by becoming an overnight, global internet sensation. At the time, I knew nothing about the internet, other than how to google. I spent my first 50 hours in training courses by internet gurus who taught me how to start and operate an online business. I took Marie Forleo's "B-School," moved on to Amy Porterfield's webinar course, then immersed myself in Russell Brunson's *DotCom-Secrets* book and joined his mastermind group.

About 18 months later, I had a blog with 40,000 faithful followers, 10,000 Facebook fans, 2 online courses for sale, and a growing coaching business. I also had the guts and the research to start this book. All within just 18 months.

Do the math. You have plenty of time. Spend 50 hours... 10,000 hours. Whatever you want. You have the time. Do not waste it believing the Lie of the Empty Hourglass.

ONLY TIME WILL TELL

Women in menopause didn't always have 30 years to burn. Until the early 1900s, the average life expectancy was below 60. So this shit is new for us. And life doesn't come with a handbook on how to be fulfilled until our mid-80s.

I would be remiss if I didn't address marital transitions here, because so many PrimeTime women I've worked with are experiencing them.

"Gray divorce" is a relatively new cultural phenomenon. According to Rosalind C. Barnett and Caryl Rivers, authors of *The Age of Longevity: Re-Imagining Tomorrow for Our New Long Lives*, overall divorce rates have begun to decline, but the rate among older Americans has more than doubled since 1990. A half-century ago, only 2.8% of Americans over 50 were divorced. Today, that figure is more than 15%, with approximately 1 in every 4 divorces occurring among couples over 50.

Technically, a gray divorce is one where both spouses are over age 50, or the marriage has lasted for more than 20 years. Gray divorce occurs for lots of reasons, but often it's the wife who pursues the split. This may be because Baby

Boomer women are the first generation where the majority joined the workforce, and they find themselves more financially independent in PrimeTime than the women who came before them. Also, marriages now have a greater number of years to withstand the stress of life. (And I've heard it quoted in more than a few articles that Viagra and Cialis have had a fair amount of impact as well. Just sayin'.)

PrimeTime is about transition. In menopause, our brains change. Our intuition becomes stronger, and we often feel more equipped to deal with "unfinished business." If you find yourself in this situation, know that you are not alone. You can google local support groups and reach out to build your own PrimeTime posse. You'll find all kinds of books on the subject as well. This shit is real, my friend. Soul sisters everywhere feel your pain and see your potential.

PrimeTime women also often experience a strong drive to contribute—to community, to charity, to society, to peace—during this time. In Chapter 13, I'm gonna hit that one hard. But just know that if you're feeling like you want to change the world, you've got plenty of time to make your mark, and plenty of PrimeTime sisters who want to do it with you. Now more than ever, the nearly 50 million women in PrimeTime are making shit happen.

PRIME RIB AND TOM PETTY

I returned to Arizona a few weeks ago to celebrate Carla's 57th birthday. We had a little party in the backyard oasis she'd created at the condo she'd bought for herself. The one with the fire pit she'd paved with broken plates to form an incredible orange mosaic. The one with the market lights strung overhead and the outdoor furniture laden with overstuffed pillows covered in fabric she'd painstakingly chosen. The one with the perfect number of tiny leopard-print touches.

We feasted on a five-pound prime rib she'd prepared in her outdoor smoker, served with au jus and homemade horseradish on the plates she'd saved from her days as a restaurateur. We drank Clicquot from long-stemmed, perfectly chilled flutes. We had laughs and sighs and a healthy dose of Tom Petty and the Heartbreakers, just like so many girl parties before. If Pauline had been there, she would have cried from pride.

Earlier that day, I'd met Carla at a house she'd recently gutted. I'd followed her five-foot-two frame, clad in size double-zero jeans with rhinestone back pockets, through mazes of two-by-four wood frames that had once been hallways. As she'd flitted and fluttered among the sledgehammers she wasn't afraid to use, the piles of broken lights and twenty-year old toilets, and the construction workers who hung on her every word, she explained to me what her creation would look like when she'd finished. On my own, I couldn't possibly have imagined it.

But in the six years since Pauline had passed, I'd seen the string of houses that had come before this one. The piles of rubbish that Carla had transformed into veritable palaces. I'd watched her become an expert. I'd witnessed how she had created stunning somethings from what appeared to be virtually nothing.

I had watched as she'd done the same with her own life.

The universe slowed down for Carla. It gave her exactly the time she needed to create her masterpiece. It gave her every bit of the time she needed to show up completely and play out her destiny. That magical look of total resolve has returned to Carla's eyes. In PrimeTime, it's more captivating than ever.

Don't tell me you're running out of time. Tell me how you'll make it work for you. This is PrimeTime, my friend. You either use it, or you lose it.

****

A couple of months after Pauline passed, Carla lovingly dismantled her closet, which had mythological status among our friends. She selected pieces for each of us. She gave me a long-sleeved t-shirt designed by Custo Dalmau from Barcelona. On the front, in shades of dark purple and fuchsia, a long-haired woman in stiletto heels straddles a motorcycle. Pauline had rocked that t-shirt at 70. Carla also gave me a pair of Pauline's pajamas—crushed velvet, giraffe print, trimmed in lime-green satin. I'm sportin' the hell out of those right now, as I write this chapter.

CHAPTER 13

The Lie of Impropriety

CROSS-COUNTRY

When I was in MBA school in my 20s, my first husband and I bought a tiny little house in San Diego. It sat on a beautiful, windy road lined with avocado and eucalyptus trees, at the base of a mountain with a cross on top. Our neighborhood had once been an artist colony, or so we were told, and the houses were tucked back from the street, hidden behind decades-old geraniums with vines like tree trunks, and bordered by ditches filled with wild calla lilies.

The single extraordinary feature of our nine-hundred-square-foot, box-shaped home was its circular driveway. It seemed as though the original architect had taken the plans and dimensions for a stately East-Coast mansion and divided them by 25. While the house was falling apart from every angle, we felt like members of the upper crest when we sat in the living room gazing through the 50-year-old warped glass of our bay window, onto that circular drive. Every now and then, when we were lucky, someone would pull up.

One night, I was studying for a finance exam while my oldest nephew sat in the living room watching TV. He was about 13 at the time, and the two of us were as thick as thieves. We both heard the motorcycle before we saw it, and we locked eyes. Then we rushed to the window to see the massive Honda Gold Wing make its way to the center of the circle. The bike was the color of a good cabernet, and I could see its heft as the front rider dropped the kickstand and leaned it slightly sideways.

I had no friends with motorcycles, so I was both curious and skeptical as the two riders climbed off. A man and a woman, both in leather chaps, black boots, and heavy helmets with face shields. Although I was clueless, my nephew recognized the woman immediately.

"I have the coolest grandma ever!" he shouted. He bolted to the front door and threw it open.

As she took off her helmet to reveal the red bandana beneath, tied do-rag style over her short black hair, Nancy laughed out loud. And I saw my mom in a way that I had never seen her before. Toned, tanned, confident, and radiant. Her eyes shone the color of the seawater in those glossy brochures that advertise vacations in French Polynesia. She stood in her full power, positively glowing, right there in our circular driveway. She was a force I will never forget.

She had ridden cross-country, nearly 3,000 miles from central Ohio to southern California, without telling any of her children she was on the way. She was 55 years old. And she was so fucking PrimeTime, I could barely take her in.

To say that I was surprised at Nancy's arrival is a gross understatement. The prior year had not been kind to her, and we all feared she might be broken for good. After the last of the kids had left the house, her 20-year marriage to my step-dad had taken a horrible turn and fallen apart. The whole process had been nasty and profoundly sad, and she was deeply scarred.

Less than six months before, she had flown out to spend two weeks with me, helping me wallpaper and paint our little house on Mollywoods Avenue. We had bonded in the way we always had: from a place of total love and zero judgment. But Nancy was forlorn and miserable. And my heart hurt for her.

What I hadn't fully realized was that once Nancy had returned home to Ohio, she made a deliberate choice. A bold and risky choice. A choice to say "Fuck you" to a world that tried to tell her how she was "supposed to" behave. A choice to do whatever the hell she wanted, in whatever way she deemed proper. A brave choice to disregard the Lie of Impropriety.

She began swing dancing. A couple of nights a week, she'd go with a girlfriend to a local bar where a DJ played honky-tonk and country rock for a dance floor packed with hard-core two-steppers. There she met a man with feet that floated, and he taught her how to own that floor. As she twirled and dipped, she felt vibrant, gorgeous, sexy, and brilliant. And for the first time in her life, she didn't care who was watching.

On that dance floor, Nancy owed nothing to anyone. She no longer paid deference to her own mother, Helen, who had grown more demanding, critical, and judgmental with age. Helen, who Nancy had moved into her home and nursed through late-stage emphysema to the end, then buried. She owed no excuses or apologies to the men she'd married, whose children she had raised before they'd tossed her aside. She owed no excuses to the seven children who had needed her and relied upon her, day in and day out, until they hadn't anymore. She had zero interest in the judgment of the high school principal, the other moms, the homeowners' association, the child psychologists, her boss, or her ex-in-laws.

On that dance floor, she was Nancy. Pure, complicated, and beholden to no one. On that dance floor, she threw her head back, she laughed, she flirted, and she *became*.

For many weeks, my mom only saw Tony-with-the-fancy-feet on that dance floor. She would show up with her girlfriend, hoping to run into him, then go home alone after an evening of honky-tonk, all smiles and sweat and sweet satisfaction. Until one morning, at a union meeting for public school system employees, when she unexpectedly spotted Tony in the crowd. Their daytime connection made their barroom experience into something real. Nancy decided to go for it.

I knew nothing about Tony until the day he climbed off that motorcycle and stepped onto our circular drive. But I loved him the moment I saw her.

THAT SHIT AIN'T RIGHT

Perhaps the most senseless and damaging of the Six Lies that Bind is the Lie of Impropriety. This lie tells us that certain behaviors, beliefs, actions, intentions, or desires are simply not proper for women "our age." I cannot begin to tell you how much this pisses me off.

But good God, we buy into it, don't we?

How many times have you stood in front of a dressing room mirror and asked yourself whether you look like you're trying too hard? If the outfit would be better suited for a younger woman? How many times have you said something like "Oh, if I were younger, I'd do that in a heartbeat!"? How many times have you watched a group of women in their 30s whooping it up and thought, "God, that looks like fun. I miss those days."

Here's the real zinger. Have you ever skipped doing something you wanted to do (or wear, or say) because you didn't want to embarrass your kids? For Christ's sake...you RAISED those kids! They had no problem embarrassing you at Denny's when they threw their scrambled eggs on the floor, now did they?

The worst part? We are told that if we begin something new and fun at midlife, if we throw caution to the wind and find our groove, we're having a crisis. A crisis, for goodness sake! I can assure you of this. When Nancy showed up at my house on that motorcycle, she was *not* having a crisis. She was having a fucking blast.

FUN AND HAPPINESS ≠ CRISIS

FUN AND HAPPINESS = THE FUTURE

Put that in your bong and smoke it, my friend! (That is, if you live in a pot-friendly state, or if you have one of those handy little medical cards.)

Think about the rules of impropriety that are binding you right now. And take a hard look at the truth. No one is in charge. No one is writing the rules. No grand scorekeeper or uber-evaluator exists. No list of approved desires hangs somewhere on an exalted refrigerator. You are in PrimeTime, which means you are a consenting adult who reports to no one. *You* are in charge. And you are highly qualified to make these decisions for yourself.

Fuck "proper." We have shit to do.

PEOPLE WON'T LIKE ME WHEN I'M HAPPY

I don't need to break down this lie the way I've broken down the others, with a whole mindset shift about the truth. Because I know that you already know the truth. You already know that "proper" is, to an amazingly large extent, a bunch of ridiculous bullshit. That it's completely subjective and different for every person. What I'm guessing, though, is that this lie keeps you from doing what you want anyway.

So think, instead, about how you proliferate the lie. How you spread it around. How you make the problem worse for yourself and other PrimeTime women. And how you can stop it, so we can all move on with the business of raising some hell.

When I coach PrimeTime women on how to fulfill their own dreams, do you know what they tell me is the number one reason they don't make moves? They are afraid of what other people will think. They tell me they are afraid of being judged by other people. This is a lie. It is the Lie of Impropriety. It sounds like this:

People won't like me if I change.

My husband or kids would disown me.

So-and-so will talk behind my back.

They'd love to kick me when I'm down.

I would look ridiculous.

It's just such a nasty little clique.

My mother (or mother-in-law) would die.

I am so afraid of what they'll think of me.

I would be proving her right.

I could write page after page of variations on this lie that I have heard from PrimeTime women. We are terrified of being judged for doing what we want to do. But the truth is that we're not afraid of what the world will think of us. We are afraid of what we will think of *ourselves*. This nasty shit comes from inside our own heads.

The number one way—the fastest, most effective, clinically proven way—to make these horrible feelings disappear is to STOP JUDGING OTHER PRIMETIME WOMEN for your own insecurities. Instead, practice complimenting them, out loud or in your mind. Practice, practice, practice.

But wait. What's that you say? You never judge? So. Much. Bullshit.

We all do it. It is human nature. But we don't all judge in the same way. Each of us judges others only through the lens of our own, uniquely specific insecurities. You only judge others based on how you judge yourself. Because it's all you can see.

Please open your mind to understanding this. Because it is a game changer, my friend.

The best explanation I've ever seen regarding this concept came from a blogger and coach named Liz Seda. She talks about the quality of metatarsal flexibility. Let me ask you some questions. Do you feel self-conscious about your metatarsal flexibility? Are you worried that people are talking behind your back about it? Your mom or your mother-in-law? Are you worried that your husband might leave you because it's not so good? Are you worried about the catty moms down at school? The ones who think their metatarsal flexibility is so fucking great? Do you fear that folks at work are standing around the water cooler, dissing your metatarsal flexibility?

I'm gonna guess that you do not. Because unless you have ever been a trained ballet dancer, you have zero idea what metatarsal flexibility even *is*. For dancers who are competing in a cut-throat world, metatarsal flexibility is essential. Your metatarsal bones connect your toes to your heels and form what's commonly known as the ball of your foot. For ballet dancers, metatarsal flexibility is a big, fucking, hairy deal.

When a ballet dancer hits an audition, if she's worried about her own metatarsal flexibility, she's also looking at everyone else's. And in her mind, she's evaluating. She's judging. She is running through a litany of "good, bad, better, she sucks, I'm fucked, or I've got this." She's also making a ton of assumptions and guesses about how other people are judging hers. It's crippling her.

Close your eyes and imagine that ballet dancer walking past you in the mall and judging your metatarsal flexibility. Think about her cruel thoughts about how the ball of your foot is too tight. Think about her harsh assumptions that the way your toes connect to your heels is horribly sub-standard. Does it hurt? Is your heart racing? Are you blushing? Fuck no. You don't give a shit, do you? Because you are not judging *yourself* on this issue.

When you tell yourself that other people will judge you because you're not behaving properly, it's a LIE. The one judging you, my friend, is *you*. Even if other people *are* thinking about you, you don't know about it! You cannot read their minds. And if you could, their thoughts could not hurt you. Thoughts are not real. They have no power. This is all absolute nonsense.

What other people think about you is none of your fucking business. But to make it past this lie—that people are judging you on what's proper—you must practice, practice, practice. And this is how you do it:

Close your eyes and choose the area of your body you are the most self-conscious about. For me, this would be my generous ass. Now imagine seeing another woman who has the same problem as you. Imagine she's wearing something that highlights this flaw. Something you would *never* allow yourself to wear.

In your mind, are you being kind and supportive? Are you saying, "God, your ass looks gorgeous hanging out like that. It's so big and so round. You look beautiful. I wish my ass were big and round like that. You are sexy as hell."

You. Are. Not.

I bet if I asked you to think of five compliments you could give that woman about the characteristic you hate about yourself, you would have an awfully hard time coming up with even one.

Because you judge yourself harshly. Then you judge other women for being like you. Then you assume that other people are judging you in that same harsh way. It's a vicious, ugly, self-perpetuated circle, this Lie of Impropriety.

Think about what you want in PrimeTime. Sit down and make a list of all the reasons you *think* someone will judge you for having it, or judge your trials and course corrections that will lead to sliding it right into your pocket. List every single one of the reasons they will criticize you, talk smack about you, see you as "less than," rank you, evaluate you unflatteringly, and generally do you wrong for pursuing what you want "at this age." Write them down!

Then own those criticisms. Because they are *yours*. They do not belong to the people who you imagine are thinking or saying them. They belong to you. Even if they did belong to those other people, those criticisms would never have any power over you, unless you were insecure about them already. Just like that ballet dancer's criticism of your metatarsal flexibility had no power over you.

Look at how cruelly you judge yourself. And make a commitment to learn to be kind to yourself. To give yourself permission to do what you think is improper. You'll learn to do that by doing it for someone else first.

Right now—today—begin a practice of complimenting other PrimeTime women for being in PrimeTime. Seek them out. Constantly be on the lookout for them. (Pay special attention to the women you already know and do not like.) In your mind, be intentionally kind to them. Encourage them. Love them. See their potential. Wish them well. Not despite the fact that they're middle-aged. But BECAUSE they're middle-aged!

Do this with strangers. Do it with the PrimeTime women who are close to you. When you are ready, stop complimenting them in your mind and start doing it out loud. This is when shit will get real. Four incredibly powerful things will happen.

1. You will meet PrimeTime women and begin to build your own posse, if you don't have one already.
2. You will stop believing the Lie of Impropriety. You will stop believing that it's not proper for you to do or have what sounds like big fucking fun "at your age."

3. You and your new posse will go out and whoop it up with reckless abandon.

4. As you live your life on your own terms, you will give the rest of us permission to do the same.

Change what's in your head, and you will change the world for PrimeTime women. Are you with me, my friend?

DAMN RIGHT

Chapter 11 might be a little late to admit this, but I swear. I cuss like a drunken sailor. If you're offended by it, please know that I mean you no disrespect. But it's not an accident. I swear for a number of wonderful reasons.

First of all, I am a serious lover of words. The bad ones, in my opinion, are some of the best ones. They are a powerful form of emphasis. They bring a point home. They help me punctuate thoughts and ideas I believe are crucial and bring color to a situation. I think they're fucking fun.

Second, I subscribed to the "good girl" rules for a hell of a long time. So swearing was the beginning of a rebellion for me. Cussing was a gateway drug for me doing whatever the Sam Hill I pleased. Once it started, it just never stopped. I don't swear in church or in board meetings or at my kid's school. And I won't swear at your house, if you don't. But this is my book, so I can do whatever the hell I please.

Third and most importantly, I swear to say "Fuck you" to the Lie of Impropriety. I swear because people would tell me that a rule exists that says I should not, and I know that's a lie. I swear because it feels good to turn my back on "supposed to." I swear because I feel powerful and independent when I make my own choices.

I swear because I burn a bridge every time I do. I burn a bridge between me and someone whose approval I would seek by pretending to be someone I'm not. I burn a bridge between me and someone who would reject me out of hand before they'd thoroughly gotten to know me. I burn a bridge between me and someone who would judge. I'm not afraid to burn those bridges, because I know that when I show up in a way that's real for me, I'll build something real with those people. They'll walk to meet me where I am, as long as I bring something valuable to the equation.

Last year, I coached a group of women through a course I called Badass Permission Slip. We had a private group on Facebook, and there the women worked together through exercises that helped them access their inner badasses. Early on, I was the only one in the group who swore. As the weeks passed, the nicest of women began to drop f-bombs here and there. Yoga teachers and spiritual healers. Schoolteachers and accountants. Graphic designers and dancers. By the end of the course, thousand-dollar cuss words were flying in every direction.

I never asked these women to do this. I'm sure that most of them didn't take the potty talk into their daily lives. But in that space, it made them feel free and rebellious and like part of a club. In that space, those words gave them a certain kind of muscle and allowed them to show an intensity they hadn't before. Those words let them try on something new and walk around in it. In that space, *we* defined what was proper.

You have every right, my friend, to decide what's proper for your own fucking life. You are a grown-ass woman. You are PrimeTime.

****

Nancy is 78 now. She's retired and lives in Arizona. We don't see one another as much we'd like. But we are still seriously tight. A couple of weeks ago, I called her on a Friday night just to chat. When she answered, I could hear shouting and singing in the background. So naturally, I asked her where she was.

She yelled, "I'm at the Mineshaft!" The Mineshaft is a pool hall with an actual swimming pool behind the bar. It's a hot spot for the local marines.

She then went on to scream, "A bunch of paratroopers are here from Belgium. I met them at a restaurant the last time they were in town, and they're back! They invited me to a birthday party. So I'm just here having the BEST time!"

I could picture Nancy there, in her yellow, button-down oxford blouse from J. Crew and her Keds. I could see her with her cane and her reading glasses and her gin and tonic. And I could imagine the paratroopers, who were probably in their 20s, who had made it a point to save her number in their phones because she's so much fucking fun. It never occurred to her or to them that a 78-year-old woman at a party with a bunch of 20-year-old soldiers was the slightest bit odd. Because Nancy doesn't live by the Lie of Impropriety. She's too damn busy doing whatever the hell she pleases.

CHAPTER 14

The Lie of Diminishing Capacity

WHAT ARE YOU TIRED OF?

My friend, Johanna, is a stunningly charming, 53-year-old, upscale hippie with a sense of humor that sets any room on fire. She has eyes the color of Ghirardelli hot chocolate and a smile that shows up before she does. I've never met a single person who knows her and doesn't like her.

Johanna works in the advertising industry, and for the past 30 years, she's helped big corporations develop their messaging. She helps them decide what to say and how to say it in a way that will make their customers sit up and listen. She's insanely good at it. She leads teams of wildly creative people. She acts as the go-between for those creative teams and the agency's clients. She's a fucking powerhouse.

It's to Johanna that I turn when I'm insecure in my own career. Because she gives it to me straight. She tells me when I'm brilliant. And she tells me when I have my head up my ass. She does this with everyone. I once heard her say to the chief marketing officer at a major global technology company, "You want it when? You're on crack. You won't have it by then, and you need to live with it, and learn to love again." Then her smile lit up the entire room.

I love Johanna for a million and a half reasons, but the biggest one is that she knows what she stands for. She is absolutely sure and confident about what she believes in. That never wavers. Emotionally, she is rock solid and seriously healthy. It's easy to be around her, because she likes being around herself.

A couple of years back, Johanna told me she was tired of her job. She didn't want to put in all the hours anymore. She said, "I'm not getting any younger, and I'm worn out." She thought it would be cool to chill a bit. You know, have some time to hang out at yoga class and pick up the dry cleaning and spend afternoons with the teenager. So she went to the brass at work and told them she wanted to work fewer hours. They offered her a 30-hour week, and they reduced her pay.

This turned out to be total bullshit for two reasons. First, she wasn't super turned on by picking up the dry cleaning, and the teenager wasn't even home in the afternoon. So she didn't experience quite the satisfaction she thought she would. Second, her schedule eventually crept right back to where it had been, and she ended up working the same number of hours as before, but for less money.

But something else turned out to be bullshit. Johanna wasn't honestly tired. She'd simply bought into one of the Six Lies that Bind: The Lie of Diminishing Capacity.

With this lie, we come to believe that we're shrinking as we grow older. We believe that our power is dwindling. That our contribution is diminished. That our abilities are moderated by age. That we are less because the years are more.

This is such a load of crap.

Johanna wasn't tired. She was tired *of* something. She had reached PrimeTime, and like so many other women, she was looking for more. She longed to make a contribution that truly mattered. She was bored. Uninspired. Without meaningful challenge.

You know those days when you feel like you could just lie down and die at lunch, but when happy hour rolls around, you magically discover a new burst of energy? Well that's exactly what happens in PrimeTime. If you let it.

For Johanna, happy hour came in the form of the 2016 presidential election. That's when she woke the fuck up. And she saw the Lie of Diminishing Capacity for the farce that it is.

Happy hour isn't the best analogy here, because Johanna wasn't happy (although she was badly in need of a cocktail). She was freaking out. The election rocked her world. She was so stunned by the campaign, so shaken by the events, so fearful for the world, so driven to DO something, that she burst out like a snake from a can in a magic show. She rode a wave of energy like I hadn't seen from her in years.

First, she sought out the players in every movement that mattered to her and got the lay of the land. Then she made signs. She marched. She recruited her friends and coworkers. She coalesced and united. One Saturday morning, she sent me a photo of herself dressed in a head-to-toe tree costume.

Then she took the next step. She volunteered at a phone bank for her political party. She joined an activist group and started attending meetings. She formed a group on Facebook and wrote her first blog post. She started thinking about what she would do with herself after she was done with the advertising world. About who she would help, how she would lead, how she could effect change over the long haul. She began reaching out to political agencies who could use her skill set and experience.

Johanna realized that what she had to give in PrimeTime was so much bigger than what she'd ever had to give before. She would no longer put words into the mouths of others. *Her* voice and *her* words would be heard. The world needed her. She would not hide in the shadows, plan for the end, or turn her back. Her beliefs were valid. Her talent and potential were real.

Johanna's capacity had not diminished with age. Quite the contrary. It had grown. She had grown. Into a force so powerful that standing next to her is like standing in a vibration.

With that new voice, she marched right back into the office of the brass and asked for her money back. Not only did they give it to her, they promoted her. She's not creating messaging for clients anymore. She's creating messaging for the agency, itself. Now she's the Chief Marketing Officer.

I saw her promotion letter. Among other things, it read "She has a giant personality and a heart to match. Jo cares about this place. She cares about all of her colleagues. She cares about her clients. She cares about the quality of our work." Damn straight, she does. She's fucking PrimeTime.

Johanna put the kibosh on the Lie of Diminishing Capacity. At 53, she's larger than life, and she's got her eye on a stack of new goals that she refuses to let go. The opposition should be very, very afraid.

BETTER THAN EVER

Although the world, and what we believe to be common sense, might tell us differently, PrimeTime often brings an absolute flood of creativity for women. By the time we hit midlife, we've been through a ton of stuff, and along the way we've picked up clues, figured life out, and gained perspective, insight, and confidence.

As our hormones shift and our bodies turn away from the roles of reproduction and protection of others, our intuition comes alight. We think differently. We innovate. We create. We originate ideas. We have business left to finish. In PrimeTime, we fucking *rock* big notions, desires, and insights. Those who would propagate the Lie of Diminishing Capacity are the worst kind of fraudsters, because they rob the world of so much juicy potential!

Our ambition generally changes in PrimeTime as well. Often it's geared toward contribution. We may feel moved to give back to our communities or to the world at large. We feel confident in our beliefs and values, and we feel compelled to share and promote them. We are creatures driven by relationships and deeper meaning, and in PrimeTime, we bring that to the world in an entirely new way.

PrimeTime women often also experience a new and deeper spirituality, and it's women in their 40s, 50s, and 60s who are leading a massive spiritual revolution in the world today.

The concept of midlife creativity—for both men and women—is supported in all kinds of research. According to Pagan Kennedy, author of *Inventology: How We Dream Up Things That Change the World,* a 2016 Information Technology and Innovation Foundation study found that inventors peak in their late 40s and tend to be highly productive in the last half of their careers. Similarly, the average inventor sends in their application to the patent office at age 47, and the highest-value patents often come from the oldest inventors, those over the age of 55. Silicon Valley may worship youth, but midlifers are making shit happen.

Not only are PrimeTime women creative and insightful, we're powerful as hell, and we have a significant impact on the health and wealth of this country. Women in general are on the forefront of purchase decisions. According to the National Association of Baby Boomer Women, 91% of all home sales in the US are driven by women, as are 60% of car sales and 51% of electronics purchases. As we enter the second decade of the twenty-first century, we are closer than ever to obtaining economic parity with men. This is something our grandmothers could have never even have fathomed. My grandmother, Helen, would have LOVED this shit!

Of the nearly 50 million women in menopause today, a good portion are from the Baby Boomer generation, which is the most influential and affluent group on the planet. The Boomers hold 90% of the net worth in the United States and 78% of the country's financial assets. And since women outlive men by 5–6 years, we'll live to see a time when 80%–90% of women are in charge of their families' financial affairs.

If you believe the Lie of Diminishing Capacity, it's time to wise up. You are part of a massive shift in power and potential. You are part of a mighty force for good, driven by collective perception, keen awareness, and a burning desire for contribution.

Don't you dare tell yourself you are small. This world needs you. I need you. This is not a time to crawl back into bed and pull the covers over your head. It's a time to be heard.

TALK IS CHEAP

The Lie of Diminished Capacity is incredibly dangerous. Because it gives us an excuse to ignore the very intuition and creative impulses that are gifted to us at this time in our lives. This lie gives us permission to say, "I'm tired" or "I just don't have the energy anymore" or "That ship has sailed for me" or "I just don't feel like it." Those are bullshit excuses.

The reason you feel exhausted, unmotivated, or uninspired is that you've spent the past 20 years of your life securing a routine. It's a goal for each one of us, isn't it? To make sure that we have every detail under control. To nail our professions, our marriages, our daily routines with our kids. To ensure that we don't have upset or crisis or chaos.

But you know what? Routine sucks. It's boring. It's fucking wearisome, my friend. You did it. You accomplished it. It worked for a while. It got you where you needed to go. But now it's time for action. It's time for a change.

Here's what's about to happen for you in PrimeTime, if it isn't happening already. As your hormones begin to shift, as your kids plan to move out—or your career hits the 25-year mark or your marriage hits its second decade or your midsection begins to spread or your intuition sets fire and ideas begin popping into your head—you will likely feel restless. You may long for transformation and change and upset.

DO NOT IGNORE THIS. DO SOMETHING ABOUT IT. Because if you simply talk to yourself (or your friends or your therapist or your husband) about this, you will waste the single biggest opportunity you've experienced since puberty!

You must ACT. In order to walk away with what you truly want, you must DO something about it.

When Johanna began to dream about what she could do to change the world, she could easily have told herself that this was a job for a younger woman. She could easily have said, "The world is a shit show, but I don't feel like fixing it.

I'm 53, for God's sake. I'm tired." But she didn't. She got off the couch and she started moving. She listened to her gut. To her intuition. To her *calling*.

If you tell yourself that your capacity is diminished— if you use this sickening lie that the world would have you believe as an excuse to ignore your desire for something new, fresh, and exciting—you will suffer. You will let yourself down. And you will let the world down.

In direct contrast to the Lie of Diminished Capacity is the truth of momentum. Momentum is the strength or force that something has when it is *moving*. It is the force that allows something to *grow stronger or faster as time passes*. It is the antidote for boredom. It is the remedy for "I'm tired." It is the solution to "I don't feel like it."

The faster an object is moving—whether it's a baseball, a car, or a toddler running away from his mother in Target— the harder it is to stop. This is also true of you and your goals. Once you begin moving and you gain some speed, you will be un-fucking-stoppable.

But momentum requires initial action. It requires you to stand up and put your intuition and desire into motion. It requires you to know that your capacity has in no way diminished. Your competence, power, aptitude, and ability are greater than they have *ever* been. But you must act in order to set them into motion and gain momentum.

One of my favorite proponents of this concept is Mel Robbins, who wrote *The 5 Second Rule*. As entertaining as she is irreverent and no-bullshit, Robbins has no problem saying that "motivation is garbage." What she so successfully teaches and promotes is the idea of acting on your desires, your impulses, or your flashes of intuition within five seconds of experiencing them. When you experience a flash of what you desire—the moment you have an idea that would facilitate change in your life—simply count down: 5–4–3–2–1, then GO. DO something about what you want. Because, according to Robbins, if you don't do it within five seconds, the idea will be gone. And you will have lost that chance.

Talk is cheap, my friend. And the Lie of Diminished Capacity is the cheapest of the cheap. You are not tired. You have not been weakened, shrunken, lessened, or devalued because of your age. On the contrary. You are about to experience an incredible shift in your life. Act, course correct. Act, course correct. Act. Tell yourself the truth about what you want. Then go out and fucking *nail it*.

THE CASE OF THE DISAPPEARING WOMAN

I wouldn't be doing my job if I wrapped up this lie before I touched on one of its ugliest consequences: the notion that PrimeTime women become *invisible*. The notion that not only do we diminish in our ability to impact the world, but we also literally vanish from sight. I cannot tell you how this sickens me.

As I was preparing my text for this chapter, Jan and I headed down to the Coast Highway for happy hour at one of our favorite spots. At the table next to us were two

PrimeTime women who were close friends. They reminded me so much of my own PrimeTime besties, as they chatted us up and shouted to be heard over the music. One of them, named Molly, asked me what I did for a living, and I told her about this book.

She said, "Oh, yeah. I need to read that. Ever since I turned 50, I've been invisible."

As she stood before me—smart, sophisticated, charming, and bubbling over with personality—in her taupe, linen dress, her Clubmaster glasses, and her trendy tennies, her significance and energy were all I could see. Invisible? WTF?

But my new friend, Molly, isn't alone.

In 2015, an herbal supplement company called A. Vogel conducted detailed research involving 2,000 women in the PrimeTime age group. A large percentage said that once they reached 51, they no longer received the level of attention that they once had. More than ⅔ of the women over 45 said they had, at one point or another, walked into a room and felt "completely unnoticed" by the opposite sex. More than half said they felt "left on a shelf" and that they'd been "judged negatively" because of their age. And more than half said that they felt intimidated by the presence of younger women at a social event.

The idea that as we grow older we become invisible is a dirty stinkin' lie. If you look at the results of the A. Vogel research, every single one of the answers specifies that the women "felt" that they were invisible. Need I remind you that MY FEELINGS ≠ FACTS. MY FEELINGS = REACTIONS

TO STIMULI? No bigger culprit—no bigger stimulus—contributes to the vicious spreading of this lie and the feelings it generates than the "anti-aging movement."

The anti-aging industry is led by companies that sell you creams and pills to recapture your youth, as though you cannot carry on happily without them. They would have you believe that the 40 years you've lived so far were better and more important than the 40 years that are yet to come. They would have you buy into ridiculous propaganda that *faking* your age—*pretending* you are younger than you are, and being perceived that way by society—will make you *feel* better.

This is an incredible crock of shit.

The anti-aging industry manipulates you into paying big bucks to eliminate any sign that you've lived a life. They spend millions to make you believe that they can restore your importance (which you never fucking lost in the first place) with a proprietary chemical compound. They operate on the lie that unless you artificially turn back the clock, you will *vanish*.

If you want to eat healthy, take bioidentical hormones, and make lifestyle adjustments so you can rock PrimeTime as optimally as possible, knock yourself out. I'll give you a standing ovation. If you want to look your best, live your best, dress your best, and act your best, then you have my best wishes.

But if you want to pretend that it's wrong for years to pass, or if you want to become a shrinking violet because they have, then I'd like to stop you right there. If you feel the need to artificially alter your age because you feel less worthy, you should know that you've been duped. I'd like to call bullshit, loudly and clearly.

I implore you to reframe your thoughts. Because you are ruining it for yourself. And when you propagate these nasty lies, you ruin it for the rest of us, too.

How can we be "anti-aging"? How can we be against something that we can't change? Are you anti-gravity? Or anti-blue sky? Being "anti" something indicates that an alternative exists. That you could *choose* a different option. The promotion of this ridiculous idea sets into motion a feeling of hopelessness and helplessness that is based 100% on manipulation.

If you buy into the bullshit idea that aging is preventable (which it's not) and horrible (which it's also not), then you will miss out entirely on the beautiful evolution that you're experiencing in this moment. You will miss out on the wisdom you've cultivated, on the value of the experiences that led you here. You will miss out on all the ways you are more beautiful, more interesting, and more nuanced than you've ever been. You will miss out on the divine opportunity that is PrimeTime. Because you will be living in the past.

From 1900 to 2007, the average life expectancy for women increased by 35 years—from 48 to 83! The miracles of modern science gave us each 35 extra years to enjoy the world! Will you really piss them away, wishing they were repeats of the ones you've already *lived*?

You are NOT invisible. I can see you. Your PrimeTime sisters can see you. The whole world can see you. It's time to show us what you've got, my friend. It's time for you to see the *truth*.

****

Johanna recruited Stacy and me to join her at the Sister March in Los Angeles in January 2017. We drove through the rain from San Diego to the Standard Hotel in downtown LA, gabbing the entire way. We spent the day before the march in the lounge, whooping it up, drinking martinis, eating french fries, telling stories, and laughing like hell. We tied one on, and we did a fantastic job of it.

The next morning, the skies opened up and the sun shone down upon us as we stepped out of the hotel lobby onto Flower Street and into the Los Angeles Financial District. We were utterly blown away by the crowd, the love, and the vibe.

And I stood in awe of my remarkable PrimeTime friend, Johanna, who was so powerfully in her element. Radiant in her beauty. Entirely at ease in her passion. Amplified by her age. Standing on the edge of what was only the beginning for her.

CHAPTER 15

Your Promotion to Brand Manager

SITTING ON THE DOCK OF REGRET

Over the past 200 pages, I've given you every reason to lean in to PrimeTime and say "Absolutely not!" to the conventional views of midlife. I've given you every reason to grab hold of what stirs your soul, trust that you've got it all going on, and rock the world along with me and millions of PrimeTime women who are busting to break out. I've given you every reason to look in the mirror, ask yourself what you want, and make it your business to make it your own.

But if you're not entirely convinced, I have one last truth you should consider before you go out and buy yourself a rocking chair.

The only feeling more powerful than the fear, anxiety, and self-reproach that keeps us from enjoying a PrimeTime that's entirely off the hook is the feeling of regret. And I'm here to tell you that you do NOT want to feel it. The loss of what might have been can be utterly excruciating.

Forgiving yourself for a bad choice is hard to do. Forgiving yourself for avoiding a potentially massive opportunity? It's gonna be brutal. And the folks over at *Psychology Today* will back me up on this one: As the years pass, and as the chance to make the right choice dwindles, that regret will evolve into rumination and chronic stress that will damage both your mind and your body.

Studies indicate that regret is more prevalent when life choices are more abundant. Those who are presented with the greatest number of opportunities are the most likely to experience the sorrow and grief that comes from not taking them. The better your PrimeTime could be, the worse you're gonna feel for not leaning into it.

A 1995 study on regret conducted by Gilovich, Medvec, and Kahneman demonstrated that regrets of inaction persist longer than regrets of action. When we say things like "I should have tried that" or "I should have asked him out" or "I should have chased my big PrimeTime dream," we are more psychologically open to conjuring up boundless possibilities for what might have been. In our imaginations, we will always live with the further riches we may have enjoyed, had we made the effort. And that imagination will serve to torture us.

In short, the pain of not doing it will far outweigh the pain of giving it a go. So join the rest of us for the party. No one ever said, "Gee, I wish I hadn't had so much fun."

POWER AND INFLUENCE

If you take away only one concept from this book, I hope you realize that you are not winding down, my beautiful PrimeTime friend. You are just getting started. Your 8:00 to 11:00 p.m. daypart should feature your best show ever, and you have the perfect training, qualifications, intuition, talent, judgment, and wisdom to generate ratings that will blow up the network.

I hope you have come to realize that midlife is a gift. A 40-year gift that was entirely unavailable to women like us only two generations ago. I hope like hell that you'll respond to that gift with gratitude, a "HELL YEAH," a fist pump, and a dirty martini.

And I hope with all my heart that from this point forward you'll look for PrimeTime women wherever you go, and that you'll lift them up, as well.

Midlife needs a rebrand. And I'm promoting you to Brand Manager. I'm giving you the critical job of educating your fellow potential superstars on the merits of rocking PrimeTime. I'm entrusting you to tell and show the world that the negativity and dread surrounding life after 45 is a complete and utter crock of crap.

Remember: A brand is nothing more than what the market *thinks of* when it hears a name or sees a label. From here on out, the world should think of *you*.

Midlife is so last century, my friend. This is PrimeTime.

Along the journey to whatever your PrimeTime heart desires, you will meet droves of women who still buy into the old brand. They're the ones who still unwittingly believe the Six Lies that Bind.

1. The Lie of Noble Selflessness: *It's wrong for me to be selfish.*
2. The Lie of Irrelevance: *I am beside the point and no longer useful.*
3. The Lie of Extenuating Circumstances: *Something is wrong with me or my life that prevents me from having what I want.*
4. The Lie of Impropriety: *That's not proper for a woman my age.*
5. The Lie of the Empty Hourglass: *I'm running out of time.*
6. The Lie of Diminishing Capacity: *I'm tired and my best days are behind me.*

But you're privy to new messaging, aren't you? You understand where this brand is going. You can show these women what they should be buying. Because you know what it means to be PrimeTime.

THE PRIME TIME MANIFESTO

This is your PrimeTime.

Your whole life has been leading to this.

You are the star of the show.

Declare what you want, with absolute certainty.

Seek what you desire, with total resolve.

Let go of the need to apologize, feel guilty, or play small.

Approach each day with the wisdom of a sage and the wonder of a beginner.

This is your PrimeTime.

Do not allow thoughts of fear, negativity, self-reproach, or doubt to hinder your quest. Your thoughts are not reality.

Do not allow your feelings to undermine your actions. Your feelings are not facts.

Do not allow your past to dictate your future. Your past is history.

Say YES to action,

…to love,

to discovery,

to chance,

to pleasure,

to challenge,

to indulgence,

to the party.

This is your PrimeTime.

Do not waste your time or your money chasing youth. The prize is in front of you, not behind.

You are perfect.

You have been given the perfect gift. Be grateful.

Trust yourself. Treat yourself. Smile at yourself and say, "Hey, Gorgeous, I love you."

This is your PrimeTime.

Stand up. Be seen. Contribute. Make waves.

Lock arms with your PrimeTime sisters. You are all connected. What stirs your souls will change the world.

Do not settle, compromise, lie down, give in, or hold back.

These days were meant to be the most thrilling, fulfilling, amusing, and astonishing of your life. Choose to make them so.

This is your PrimeTime.

It is the time of your life.

And you are everything.

Look, the world needs you. I need you. Your PrimeTime sisters need you. But don't do it for us. Do it for yourself. Do it so that when you finally do hit that Late News daypart, you have something big and juicy to report. Do it so you can deliver the biggest bombshell of the century. Do it because you were *meant* for it. Do it because you're PrimeTime.

I'M SO PROUD TO STAND BESIDE YOU

The morning I marched with Johanna and Stacy, a total of 93,000 women had registered on Facebook and estimates state that between 400,000 and 750,000 women showed up.

When we left our hotel, we stepped into a sea of women that spanned dozens of blocks. I was gifted one of the most significant and moving experiences of my adult life. Not because I rallied against something, but because of the absolute *opposite*.

I stood alongside my sisters that morning. I locked hands with women of all shapes, colors, sizes, ages, and beliefs. Together, we generated a collective energy so powerful, so thoughtfully cultivated from love, so passionately driven by hope, so soulfully inspired by tolerance, that I cried repeatedly.

So many women attended the march that we were unable to physically move forward. We had nowhere to go. The streets were filled from sidewalk to sidewalk. So we stood. We stood in unity. We stood in harmony. We stood in strength.

As I looked around, I saw my PrimeTime future. I saw the unrelenting splendor and potency of women. I saw that it would be my divine privilege, and my duty, to serve. I saw *you*. And in that moment, I fell in love.

References

Barnett, Rosalind C., and Rivers, Carol. *The Age of Longevity: Re-Imagining Tomorrow for Our New Long Lives.* Lanham, Maryland. Roman and Littlefield. 2016

Branden, Nathaniel. "What Self-Esteem Is and Is Not." http://www.nathanielbranden.com/what-self-esteem-is-and-is-not

Browne, Harry. *How I Found Freedom in an Unfree World, A Handbook for Personal Liberty (25th Anniversary Edition.)* LiamWorks. 1998

CenterforDiseaseControl.https://www.cdc.gov/nchs/data/databriefs/db232.pdf

Chopra, Deepak. *Perfect Health, The Complete Mind and Body Guide.* New York: Three Rivers Press. 1991.

Crowe, Sheryl. Trott, Jeff. MacLeod, Brian. "Every Day is a Winding Road." Album: Sheryl Crow. A&M. 1996

Ehrmann, Max. *The Poems of Max Ehrmann*. Viquesney Publishing Co. 1906.

Gates, Bill. *The Road Ahead*. Penguin Books. 1995.

Gilovech, Medvec and Kahneman. "Varieties of Regret, A Debate and Partial Resolution." *Pyschological Review*, Vol. 105 No. 3. 1998

Greenberg, Melanie, PhD. "The Psychology of Regret." 2012. PsychologyToday.com/blog/the-mindful-self-express /201205/the-psychology-regret

Hay, Louise. "What is Mirror Work?" http://www.louisehay. com/what-is-mirror-work/

Katie, Byron. *Loving What Is, Four Questions that Can Change Your Life*. New York: Harmony Books. 2002.

Kennedy, Pagan. *Inventology: How We Dream Up Things That Change the World*. Wilmington, MA: Mariner Books. 2016

National Association of Baby Boomer Women. "Free Resources." https://nabbw.com/

Pressfield, Steven. *Do the Work: Overcome Resistance and Get Out of Your Own Way*. The Domino Project and Do You Zoom, Inc. 2011

Robbins, Mel. *The 5 Second Rule – Transform Your Life, Work, and Confidence with Everyday Courage*. New York: Savio Republic. 2017

Seda, Liz. "How to Free Yourself from Fear of Judgement." http://www.alifeonyourterms.com/how-to-free-yourself-from-fear-of-judgement/

Shaw, George Bernard. *Mrs. Warren's Profession.* 1893

World Life Expectancy. http://www.worldlifeexpectancy.com/usa/life-expectancy-female

Acknowledgements

I am deeply thankful to the following people for their support, their inspiration, and their encouragement. This book would not have been possible without them.

To my mom, Nancy, who told me from the moment I first opened my eyes that I could do anything. To Jan Bretschneider, my one and only true love, for believing in me, investing in my dreams, and having my back in every moment. And to Christian, for allowing me to co-op his story as my own, and for being the best kid who ever lived. Thanks, as well, to my brothers, Allen, Ted, Tom, Bryan, Shawn, and Brady, who humored my delusions of grandeur and allowed me to operate as a princess for so many years. And to my Dad, Delino Eugene, who taught me that bullshit is a bona fide talent, and that I was graced with it. He would be so proud of me if he were alive. To the amazing women of my family: Shelly, Delfia, Debbie, and Lori, who hold it all together. And to my Bretschneider family: Christian, Sigrid, Grit, Mahmoud, and Samir, who took me in, loved me, and made me world-wide.

Thank you to my amazing girl posse: Stacy, Johanna, Jo Lia, Heather, Carla, Gina, Tammy, Shani, and Elena. When times are really good, and when times are really bad, these are the girls I want to hole up with. You make me better, and you make me laugh. And to the boys: Danny B, Scooby, Woody, Rono, Anthony, Artie, Eric, Joe, Norm, Adam, Jonathan, and Axel. For loving me, and for making me brave.

Special thanks to Russell Brunson and to Coach Mandy Keene, who encouraged me to climb to the top of the mountain and plant my flag, and forbade me to quit. And to the members of the Inner Circle who led me through the writing and publishing process: Ken Dunn, Julie Eason, and Nicolas Silvy. I am so grateful for your counsel and your genius. To Arthur Tubman, who called me out and told me that I'd never be happy until I stepped fully into my calling. And to Bryan Bowman and Yara Golden, who cheered me on and humored me as I bitched, moaned, and doubted. And a special shout out to my wonderful editor, Julia Wilson, who made my words sing.

And many thanks to the amazing Megan, who lived my life while I lived inside these pages, and who cheered for me day-in and day-out.